the Planner Book

the Planner Book

STYLISH PROJECTS TO CREATIVELY ORGANIZE AND COMMEMORATE THE DAY TO DAY

Jean Sagendorph
and Dawn DeVries Sokol

St. Martin's Griffin
New York

www.stmartins.com

The Library of Congress Cataloging-in-Publication Data is available upon request.

ISBN: 978-1-250-17685-1 (trade paperback)

Our books may be purchased in bulk for promotional, educational, or business use. Please contact your local bookseller or the Macmillan Corporate and Premium Sales Department at 1-800-221-7945, extension 5442, or by email at MacmillanSpecialMarkets@macmillan.com.

First Edition: July 2018

10 9 8 7 6 5 4 3 2 1

See page 185 for a continuation of the copyright page.

Contents

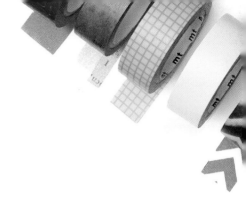

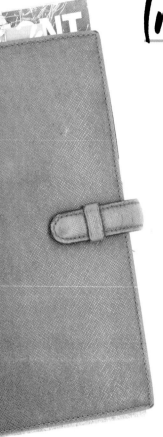

Introduction

Like many people, I love my cell phone. A few years ago I was met with some (massive) personal challenges—better known as Debt, Divorce, and Moving—and I couldn't manage all of these challenges on just a phone, so I returned to my first love: paper. Initially I used a notebook from my sister's ample stash, but I longed for an old-school planner. I desperately wanted a cobalt blue Filofax, but they're pricey, even on eBay, and budgeting was my main goal. One day, total dumb luck, I was tag sale-ing with a friend in the Woodstock area and there it was: Old Bluey! I asked how much and was told $2. I almost cried. The tool she so readily sold to me helped change my life.

Using paper helped me not only to organize my time, it aided me in the process of rethinking what was important to me and where I wanted my life to go now that I was an official adult (in my 40s; I'm a late bloomer). The planner gave me a daily sense of accomplishment, even if it was only checking off "buy milk" or "take out trash." And I enjoyed pasting pics that my nieces drew for me into the planner. It became one part organizer, one part diary.

I don't have beautiful handwriting—my sisters got all of that talent—nor do I have the ability to sketch crowd-pleasing landscapes, but my planner was a window into a world where I could control my limited time, create lists for my overtaxed brain, and remind myself to hit the gym. More importantly, it helped me create a path to get where I needed to be, both short term and long term. It also allowed me to put the brakes on my goals when emergencies happened, and then shift back into gear when it was appropriate. As I write this introduction in the Saratoga Springs Public Library, I'm six weeks away from moving into my dream home. It turns out my dream home isn't

a penthouse in New York City or a fancy mansion, but a cottage on a lake. By using my planner, I realized that I didn't want to spend time managing stuff (and I assure you, I like stuff). Instead, I want to spend that time on artistic pursuits, hiking, kayaking, traveling, and honestly, having a beer with friends and family. To get there, I needed to eliminate more debt than most people can imagine (divorce will do that to you) and protect my business. That meant I had to sell my fancy house—including tag selling, donating, or giving away about twenty-five percent of my possessions—and then find a tiny and very cheap cottage on a lake. It took nearly five years of organizing my chaotic life while I worked three jobs (as a writer, literary agent, and free-lancer) and renovated and sold my house, but it happened. The cottage on a lake turned out to be an A-frame that I bought for a little less than $34,000 in December 2017. Renovating it has created pages upon pages of notes and other information that I carry around in my planner and in a folder. It's 1,016 square feet of happiness with very little overhead.

Someone once called me a Progress Junkie. I wear it like a badge of honor.

I've worked with Dawn Sokol on a number of books over the years, so when I approached her to see if she might be interested in working on a book about creating planners I felt confident that we would have a great adventure, and we have. We've more than bridged the agent/client relationship over the years, and I think of her as a very dear friend. Really, to hear her laugh on our many conference calls is a joy. The fact that she didn't sweat it when I needed to take a step back for a few weeks when my brother-in-law was ill is a testament to our ability to plan, the trust in our friendship, and the mutual respect we have for each other's artistic vision. I couldn't ask for a better partner on this project.

We also knew we'd need someone to help us organize all of the contributors as well as cross the i's and dot the t's, or rather cross the t's and dot the i's, and so Michelle Witte joined our merry band, and here we have the book.

I hope you'll be pleased that nearly all of the projects can be completed with everyday items and scaled up using luxury goods or scaled back using odds and ends found at dollar stores or in your junk drawer. Most of all, I hope you create a tool that you look forward to using and that helps you set your sights on your dream and carve out a path to turn that dream into a goal and, eventually, a reality.

Next on my list:

❑ Hire movers
❑ Unpack
❑ Petfinder.com

—Jean Sagendorph

Introduction

When I was a full-time book designer I made a lot of lists: lists of sections in the book with corresponding page numbers, pages that still needed to be designed, what had been designed as final, etc. Now that I work as an author who only designs her own books, I don't have as many design projects happening concurrently. But I still keep my lists—and my schematics.

What is a schematic, you ask? It's kind of like a storyboard for the book designer. It's a way to format the book to see what's going where so you can figure out the flow of the book. When my coauthor, Jean, saw the first schematic I filled in for *The Planner Book*, she told me she knew what I had to write about for my introduction.

"It's a planner," she said.

She's right. It is a planner, but I never thought of it that way. I didn't see myself as a planner sort of gal—more of an art journaler—but planning is in my blood. I graduated with a degree in journalism, and deadlines are still extremely important to me. So I make lists. When I get into the nitty-gritty of a deadline and it feels overwhelming, I create lists and schematics.

The schematic is never pretty. It's basically boxes with the titles of projects and parts of the book, written in pencil so it can easily be erased, with yellow highlighter X's to show the pages that have been designed and sent to the editors. Yellow dots in upper left corners signify pages that have been designed but are not totally solidified in their spots. Boxes with half an X are where content has been placed, but we're still waiting on one small piece of the puzzle. Page numbers can change, up until the very end of the deadline. Maybe the editors decide it doesn't flow and move some projects around. Maybe a

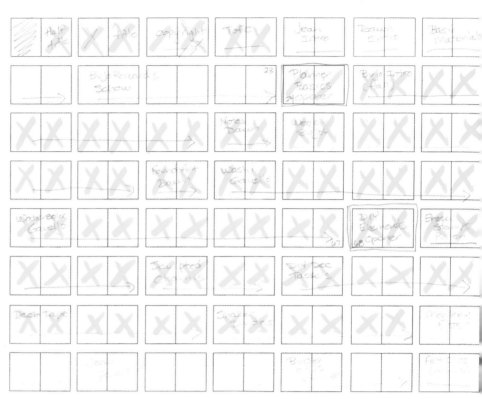

The schematic for this book once the first section, "Planner Basics," was mostly designed. It ain't pretty!

project runs longer than what I had anticipated, so page numbers shift. Let me put it this way: The table of contents page is never finished until all the rest of the pages are X'd on that schematic. Unfortunately, after constant erasing, no amount of Washi tape, cool lettering, or anything fancy will make it appealing. It is what it is.

It's kind of funny: I live by the schematic. Yes, I'll make lists in my daily planner of pages I want to design on certain days, or lists of what still needs to be edited before I format it into the book, but the schematic is my lifeline. Once I see all the boxes filled in with those full X's, I take a deep breath and think about the next project or book coming down the pike. And I look forward to penciling in my next schematic.

—Dawn DeVries Sokol

Basic Materials

COVERING THE NUTS AND BOLTS
OF YOUR SUPPLY STASH

Every craft book starts out with a materials section, listing the ins and outs of all the tools and doodads you'll need to create the projects within the pages. This book is no exception, but with one point added: To plan, you really don't need any of them.

What?! What's that you say? Well, OK, we've got your attention. To plan your day, yes, you'll need a planner. Yes, you'll need the bare-bones basics.

But you want your planning experience to go further. You are a planning enthusiast. You dream in lined or graph paper, you outline your daily life with decorative tape. Cute paper clips and rubber stamps call your name. We've got just the book for you.

We are going to show you how to make your own cute paper clips,

your own decorative tape, and your own doodads. For those projects, you'll need a few items in your arsenal. Some of them you might already have; others are easily acquired, and the more specific ones we will list in our Resources section. Listed below are the bare minimum:

The Ideal Planner

Yep, you'll need a planner. In the final project section of the book, we offer up six projects to create a planner of your own. But any will do. Whichever is your preference.

Writing Tools
PENS AND PENCILS

Any writing implement will do—ballpoint pens, felt-tip pens, colored pencils, Number 2 pencils… Try a few different kinds and see what works for you. We like Sakura Microns for a smooth black line that doesn't bleed through most paper.

Adhesives

GLUE

White, epoxy, gel medium—most glues that you have on hand will probably work.

TAPE

Washi, Scotch, two-sided, duct, masking—there are all kinds of tape. Roller adhesives, such as Tombow MONO Adhesive, stick decently and travel well. Repositionable (temporary) adhesives are good for when you want to play with your pages but don't want to make them permanent just yet.

Ruler

Any straight edge will do, as long as it's sturdy and shows measurements.

Scissors

So many scissors, so little time! It's good to have a small pair in your arsenal for those wee bits you need to cut, like cutouts of photos, small shapes, etc.

Hole Punch

Hole punches just keep getting fancier. There are large ones, like the Crop-A-Dile by We R Memory Keepers, that reach further, punch different-size holes, and even set eyelets.

Old Books

Find 'em on eBay, in bargain bookstores, at estate sales, and flea markets.

Paper of Varying Weights

Enough said!

Needle and Thread

Most variations will suffice.

Buttons

Fabric Scraps

Felt, cotton, old denim jeans that don't fit anymore . . . anything will work! Ribbons and trim are good to have, too.

Paint

Watercolor pan paints travel well, as do watercolor pencils. Acrylics, such as craft paints, are great, too!

Rewards of Planning

GOING FROM DREAMING
TO PLANNING TO ACHIEVING

By Betsy Schow

I have a confession: I used to hate planners. They seemed so judgy. The blank spaces taunted me, telling me that I needed to fill each line with things to do. If I left any part empty, I was lazy at best, useless at worst. I wasn't doing enough. I wasn't enough. So in an attempt to change that, I would throw myself into new goals with excitement and determination:

• Lose that 75 pounds
• Make homemade cards and memory books for my children
• Learn to quilt and sew my own dresses

I tried, I really did. Unfortunately, without a plan, the motivation from my starter's high faded and my determination fizzled into nothing until I inevitably quit. Which was exactly how I ended up depressed and obese with a garage full of about a thousand dollars in scrapbook supplies, boxes of fabric, and a sewing machine that I'm absolutely sure was possessed by a vengeful demon intent on snarling thread and sewing through my thumb.

Haunted craft supplies aside, seven years ago a few things happened in my life that changed everything. One fall, I started yet another diet attempt that was doomed to fail. Except it accidently turned into an unbelievable year of conquering my fears and learning how to finish my goals and love myself in the process. I discovered that what had weighed me down all my life wasn't the excess pounds but rather the weight of all the goals I had made and abandoned. That change in perspective gave me control of my life and transformed me into a finisher rather than a quitter, and helped me develop the philosophy of finishing that formed the basis of my book *Finished Being Fat*.

However, even after those experiences I still hated planners. I figured I didn't need them. I was the unstoppable Finishing Diva. I could make and keep any goal without help. Nothing was impossible. No marathon too long. No mountain too big.

Until one day life happened.

My daughter had always been a challenge, but as she got older her tantrums grew louder and longer. Over the years we took her to doctors and therapists for help. One day we finally received a diagnosis: Autism with a Disregulatory Mood Disorder. Suddenly my life went from keeping my goals to keeping my daughter safe. She had become the sun, because my whole world now revolved around her.

Anyone who has worked with a child on the Autistic Spectrum knows that the key to survival is structure, routine . . . and a box of chocolate or a glass of wine at the end of the day. Finally, after trying and failing to keep track of all her therapies and behavior interventions, in addition to my own training and goals, I decided to confront my old enemy—the planner.

My first planner was gorgeous and complicated . . . and utterly useless. To be honest, it was meant entirely for show—to make myself feel good about using some of those scrapbook supplies from the garage and to give me a sense of accomplishment for finishing all the things I had listed on those daily planner pages. But that was the problem; I'd put in so many things that there was no way to get them all done on the best of days, and I certainly didn't account for life's little interruptions or the rough days. Instead of the planner making my life easier, the days got harder while I felt miserable, worried that I was failing myself and my daughter. The proof was right there in my own handwriting. Set in stone. All the things I needed to do but failed to cross off the list.

The stress and the pressure kept building, and eventually a panic attack hit me in the middle of day. I fled to my room and buried myself under as many blankets as I could find. I could still hear my daughter wailing "Mom!" at the top of her lungs because she needed me to find the paint supplies so she could presumably make some manner of creative masterpiece that I would inevitably have to clean up.

Eventually she tracked me down and burrowed into my sanctuary. As soon as she saw my crying face, she stopped her demands and stared in confusion. I could see the gears working in her head as she scurried off to grab her feelings chart—a colorful paper with a list of emotions and their matching faces. Since those with autism have difficulty reading facial expressions and identifying feelings, the therapists had made us a simple chart so my daughter could learn to recognize her own feelings and the feelings of others. Only then would she understand and respond accordingly. After she grabbed the chart off the living room wall, she invaded my blanket fort again and pointed to a blue frowny face emoji on her laminated chart.

"You are having a sad day," she said matter of factly. "Why?"

I shrugged. Sure I was having a tough time, but there was nothing I could do about it. Life kept moving on and I had to run to keep up with it, no matter how I felt.

My daughter patted my arm, more like an old woman than an eight-year-old. "Some days are bad. I will find the paints this time, but you have to get my foods out when you have a happy day. Deal?" She didn't wait for an answer and wriggled away.

I sat there for a little longer, both ashamed that I couldn't keep myself together in front of my child and awed that my daughter was able to identify that I was having a hard time. And beyond that, she responded to me with compassion, giving me permission to take it a little easy while things were overwhelming—which was something I'd never managed to give to myself.

She gave me exactly what I needed.

To be honest, I think a lot of people need the same thing: Compassion for ourselves. Flexibility to not be at our best 24/7. Permission to admit that some days are craptastic and we don't get to choose when those days hit us upside the head.

The Feelings Planner

Thus began the first planner I didn't hate. It's a book where, instead of listing and planning out everything I had to get done, it's a companion to help me identify the tough days and keep myself on track to meet my goals anyway. The concept is very simple and a spin on the Philosophy of Finishing I had already discovered:

Not everyone can win the race, but everyone can finish. So run when you can. Walk if you need to. Crawl when you have nothing left. Just keep moving and you WILL get to the end.

With that mantra in mind, I planned to meet my goals—both small projects that only took a few weeks and big goals that were a main focus for the year (run a marathon, maintain a healthy weight, remodel the house). The key was to break them down into more manageable monthly, and even weekly or daily, focuses.

I'll use myself as an example. During the past two years I'd stopped paying attention to what I ate, how much I exercised, or how much I slept. In light of everything else going on, it didn't seem important. Now I realized that my own well-being was the foundation for everything, and I was ready to get that back on track. Something that couldn't happen overnight but needed to be achieved day by day.

So each month I would start off by listing the steps that would get me closer to my goal. For example:

• By the end of the month I want to be making most of my own meals.

or

• By the end of the month I want to be able to run a 5k.

Once I had those minor goals established I got into the real work—the daily tasks that would get me there. If I'd written good monthly goals, it was pretty easy to simplify the goals into tasks.

• Make my own dinner.
• Exercise for an hour.
• Get to bed by ten.
• Stay away from sugar.

This was all well and good, but I also had to be honest with myself—some days I would be able to mark off each one of those tasks, but some days I would be super lucky to get a shower. Building off my daughter's feelings chart, I figured out how to identify and accommodate those days and still be able to move forward with the mindset that there's no chance of failure.

To keep me on track and achieve my goals, I decided to use a simple point system. Each week I had my list of tasks that would get me closer to my goal. Each task was worth one point, whether it was running five miles or meditating for a half hour. The next part was pretty much entirely my daughter's brainchild. You see, once she saw what I was doing, she decided I should have a similar system to the one we used to reward her for identifying her feelings and improving her behavior. So she decided mommy needed big emoji stickers like hers that I could use in the planner to help me decide what sort of day I was having.

The giant smiley sticker
These were the days I felt great and I could do whatever I set my mind to— the sky was the limit, so I should get three or more points while I felt great.

The thumbs-up sticker
For the days I was doing okay enough that I could handle most of the things that needed doing—meaning I needed to accomplish at least two tasks of the weekly list for two points.

The poo emoji sticker
My daughter's favorite sticker because, well, she's eight. But I find the imagery fitting, because some days are craptastic and plans go awry. On those days, sometimes I needed to force myself, but I was able to do at least one thing to move forward to my goal, even if it was just self-care and mindfulness.

Now that I had my weekly tasks and three types of days with suggested daily points, I needed to figure out the minimum weekly point total that would keep me on track for my goals. Through trial and error, I settled on twelve points, meaning at some time during the week I needed to do at least twelve tasks. My daily points and tasks were never consistent—heck, some days it meant pulling out the Chinese takeout menu instead of preparing a homemade meal. But as long as I was meeting my weekly point total I knew I was still doing great and making progress.

Though the system was tweaked, we used the same point idea for my daughter. It helped her see the progress she was making and get rewarded for improving. It helped me chart where she was in her emotions and treatment. If her point total was much higher than twelve, she had an awesome week and was ready for more responsibility next week. Likewise, if I was constantly over-scoring my weekly total, then I needed to make my weekly tasks harder. On the opposite end of the spectrum, if my daughter or I got under twelve points total for the week, maybe we were trying to do too much. Consistently getting under twelve week after week meant something was wrong and we needed to reevaluate how hard our tasks were. With this system, I'd given myself permission to do just that—to alter my plans as needed when life happens, as it inevitably does.

Success or failure is a choice and really a matter of perspective. Forget what sounds impressive, how much your perfect neighbor gets done, or how much you think you should be doing. Because good day or bad, the important thing is to just keep moving forward. Whenever I have doubts, I watch my daughter and the joy that lights up her face when she realizes she got enough points for the week. That sense of achievement is priceless yet worth everything.

A goal is like a finish line. The line doesn't change, even when my path to get there needs to. I might need to take the scenic route, I might be fast or slow, but I will get there. My daughter will get there.

And so will you.

About the contributor

Betsy Schow's philosophy of finishing has been featured in *The Wall Street Journal*, the *TODAY* show, and the *Jenny McCarthy Show*, among others. She is the author of *Finished Being Fat* and *The Quitter's Guide to Finishing*, as well as the young adult *The Storymakers* series. When Betsy isn't writing, you can find her running around Baltimore, raising her special-abled child, and working with the nonprofit children's organization, Odyssey of the Mind.

You wrote a book called *Finished Being Fat* about going from a sedentary life to running a marathon. Was there one specific moment that changed you from "wanting" to "doing"?
There were several "aha!" moments which made me realize that my perspective was skewed. A big moment was after I lost twenty pounds, I stayed up all night sobbing, panicked because I knew the weight would come back. All I could see was myself as a failure. It was then that I realized perception is reality. My perception was that I was a loser and a quitter, so that was my reality. If I wanted to be different, I needed to change not only what I did, but how I looked and talked to myself. Change your perception, change your reality.

Many of us lack discipline. Any tips on how to pick ourselves back up to try again?
So much of discipline is mental and how you look at it. In the beginning of my journey, I looked at life like a race. Later, I decided to shift to a mental image of climbing a mountain. In a race I'm competing with others, but with a mountain, there's only me and the summit. If I fall, I have two options: stay on the ground and rot or stand and move forward one more step. Then another. And another. I try to remember when things suck that the highest mountains have the prettiest views.

In *The Quitter's Guide to Finishing*, you discuss the difference between a dream and a goal. Can you give us a short recap?
Put simply, both are changes or things you want. A dream relies on other people, luck, timing, and things out of your control. If you focus on a dream, you could do everything right but still not reach your desired outcome. A goal is based on your actions. You control the outcome. Not fate. Not luck. Just you. It's the difference between winning a marathon and completing one. You can control if you keep moving forward, but you can't help how fast the other guys are.

Planner Basics

SIX PROJECTS TO GET
YOU STARTED, NO MATTER
YOUR SKILL LEVEL

You can jump to any project in the book but we specifically chose these projects for the beginning because they will give you both a great introduction to setting up your first planner (especially if you're interested in bullet journal style) and also get your feet wet with the creative side of using your planner with watercolor, markers, washi tape, doodling, or repurposing items around your house.

Datum / Date:

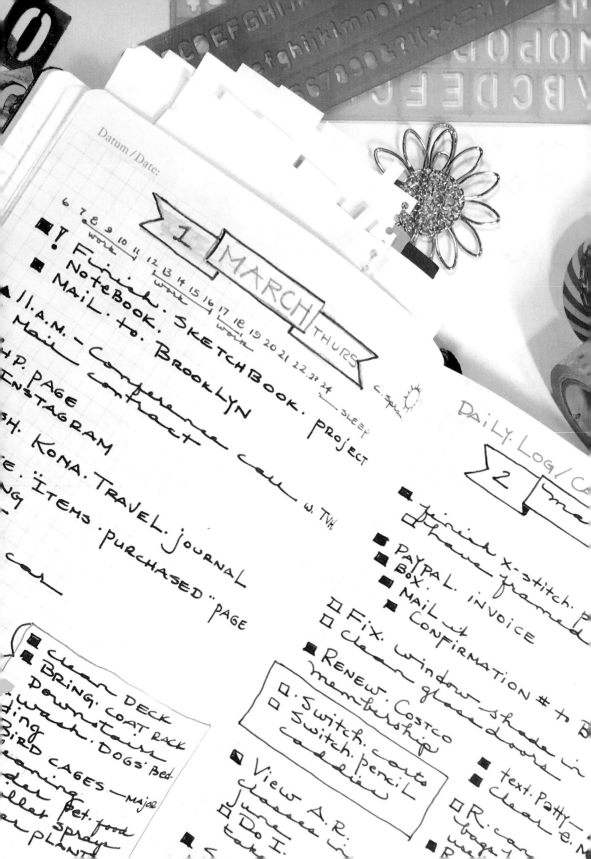

6 7 8 9 10 11 12 13 14 15 16 17 18 19 20 21 22 23 24
work   work   work   sleep

1 MARCH THURS   C. Spls ☼

- ■ ! Finished. Sketchbook. Project
- ■ Notebook.
- ■ Mail. to. Brooklyn
- ▲ 11. A.M. – Conference call w. TVH
- ▲ Mail contract
- ▲ H.P. Page
- ▲ Instagram
- ● SH. Kona. Travel. Journal
- ● Items. Purchased " page

DECK
- ■ Clean. DECK
- ■ Bring. Coat Rack
- Downstairs
- wash. Dogs' Bed.
- ... Bird cages — major
- ... pet. food
- ... spray
- ... plant

DAILY. LOG / Ca

2 Ma

- ■ Finished X-stitch. P
- □ Phone. framed
- ■ Paypal. invoice
- ■ Box.
- ■ Mail it
- Confirmation # to B
- □ Fix. window shade in
- □ Clean. glass doors
- ■ Renew. Costco
- Membership
- □ Switch. coats
- □ Switch. pencil
- Caddie
- ■ View. A.R.
- classes in
- Do I.

- ■ text. Patty—
- clean e.m.
- □ R. car

Skill Level: *Beginner* • Budget: *Varies*
Time: *Varies*
Contributor: *Theresa Hall*

The Basics of Bullet Journaling

Keeping a bullet journal isn't time-consuming or difficult. The time spent on a bullet journal differs from person to person. It all depends on your life and needs.

Introduction to Bullet Journaling

The original bullet journal planning system is the creation of Ryder Carroll. Commonly referred to as a "BuJo," a bullet journal is a visual reminder of your tasks and events, aiding you in identifying and focusing on the things that are truly worth your time. It is easy to customize to your specific needs. Best of all, you can't do it wrong!

The bullet journal differs from other methods, because it's a planner, a collection of to-do lists, and a journal all in one. I've been using this method for years because it tracks my daily activities and goals, as well as my experiences each day. It is a log of my life.

SUPPLIES NEEDED:
NOTEBOOK
PEN OR PENCIL

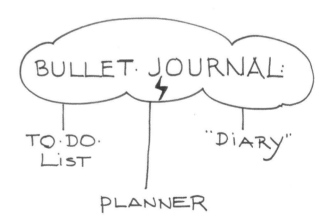

Instructions

In this guide, I've simplified the concepts and setup, but this method can be tailored to fit your specific needs. If you're new to bullet journaling, I recommend watching the video by Ryder Carroll, which can be found at www.bulletjournal.com.

SETUP AND EXPLANATION: THE BASIC ELEMENTS OF A BULLET JOURNAL

The basic elements of a bullet journal are:

Index
Future Log
Monthly Log
Daily Log
Bullets
Signifiers

INDEX

The first four pages of your new journal will be your INDEX.

Number each page, at the top or bottom, depending on your preference. Leuchtturm 1917 and the Official Bullet Journal (produced by Leuchtturm 1917) come with the pages already numbered. How convenient!

While it can take some time to number each page, doing so will come in handy. Each time you begin a page in your journal, write a TOPIC at the top of the page—such as "Birthday Plans." Then go to your Index and write down "Birthday Plans." Write down the page number(s) that correspond with that topic. By assigning each page a number and a Topic, and entering them in your Index, you will be able to find your

SELECTING A NOTEBOOK

Size is important when it comes to the notebook you choose to use for your bullet journal. If it's too small, you could quickly run out of room. Likewise, if it's too large it might not be comfortable to carry with you daily.

Try notebooks like Leuchtturm 1917, Moleskine, Piccadilly, or an inexpensive composition tablet—any will do. There is also an official Bullet Journal notebook produced by Leuchtturm. A composition notebook can be purchased for as little as a dollar, while the Leuchtturm 1917 and Moleskines can be anywhere from $14 or more. When you purchase more expensive notebooks, you are paying for the quality of the notebook and the paper itself. High-quality paper is a pleasure to write on. I archive all my filled journals, so using good, thick paper that holds up over time is very important to me.

Whichever notebook you choose for your bullet journal, make sure it's a pleasure to use. You'll be writing in it often.

information quickly instead of having to look through your entire journal.

FUTURE LOG

The FUTURE LOG, or Yearly Log, is a quick look at events in the months ahead. It is like the main page of your twelve-month calendar.

Set aside the next four pages after the Index to create/draw your Future Log. Take each page, divide it into three sections, and write the name of the month on each section. You can do this freehand or by using a ruler.

Section one is "January," section two is "February," and so on, until each section has been assigned a month. This is your Future Log, where you'll write important events (such as birthdays and anniversaries) that you want to be able to see easily and quickly.

MONTHLY LOG

The MONTHLY LOG is simply your month at a glance.

Start your Monthly Log by writing the name of the month at the top of your new page.

SELECTING A WRITING UTENSIL

I prefer to use a fountain pen in my bullet journal because it makes me concentrate on my tasks while also exercising my handwriting skills. I love how a fountain pen writes on good-quality paper, so it's almost a pleasure to jot down errands and notes.

Keep in mind that pencil can fade over time. Remember, it's your planner/journal, so go with your preference.

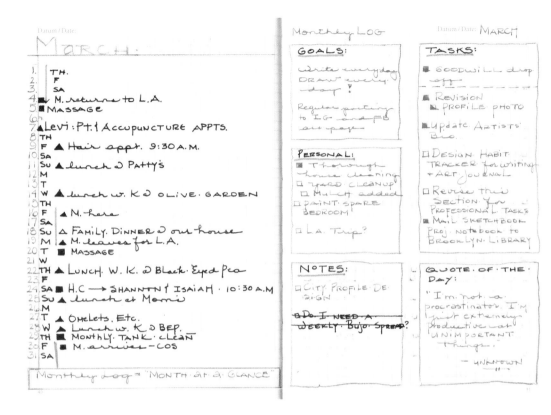

Below that write the days of the month, "1, 2, 3 . . ." There should be one day per line. Next to the number, write the corresponding day of the week (S, M, T, W, TH, F, SA).

Here you can write a monthly task, bills due, a project deadline, etc., on the day of the month they're due.

Refer back to your Future Log for that month and enter any important events in your Monthly Log.

On the opposite page of your Monthly Log, you can write notes, actions, lists, etc., that pertain to that month. Because you are using the BuJo method in a blank notebook, you are not limited to how many pages you can use or where you can begin your month. With the Monthly Log in place, the next page will be the start of your Daily Log.

This is important: Because you may not know how many pages you'll need for the current month, only create the next Monthly Log at the end of the month you're in.

DAILY LOG

Finally we come to The DAILY LOG.

The Daily Log is just your daily calendar page.

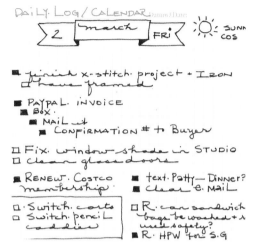

DAILY. LOG / CALENDAR Date/Day/Date

2 march FRI SUNN COS

- finish x-stitch project + IRON
  I have framed
- PAYPAL. INVOICE
  - BOX.
    - MAIL it
      - CONFIRMATION # to Buyer
- FIX. window shade in STUDIO
- Clean glass doors
- RENEW. COSTCO   - text. Patty — Dinner?
  membership.   - Clean e. MaiL
- Switch. carts   R. can sandwich
- Switch. pencil   bags be washed + r
  caddies   used safely?
                       - R. HPW for S.G

I begin the first day of my Daily Log on, you guessed it, the first day of the month. And I start it only after I'm satisfied that I am ready to move on from the Monthly Log page(s) of the previous month.

I begin by writing the day of the week, and the date at the top of the next blank page. Because it interests me, I write the current weather and temperature at the top of the page too. The Daily Log is where you write down the events, tasks, and appointments and notes that are relevant to that one particular day. Some BuJo users track how many glasses of water they've

consumed on that day too. It's their BuJo, so why not?

BULLETS AND SIGNIFIERS
BULLETS are the tasks, events, and notes that you record in your journal.

SIGNIFIERS are symbols that give you quick information and context for each bullet at a glance. Keep in mind, not all bullets need signifiers.

KEY TO SIGNIFIERS
Here is a Key to the Signifiers and their meanings, some as created by Ryder Carroll and some I modified for my needs. To help me remember what each signifier means, I write them on a card and use it as a bookmark in my bullet journal. (They are shown in the photo below.)

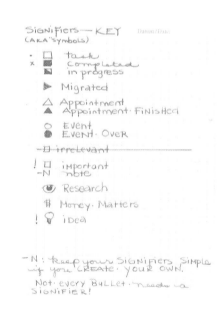

SIGNIFIERS — KEY   Date/Day/Date
(AKA "symbols")

- ☐ task
x ■ Completed
  ◪ in progress
▶ Migrated
△ Appointment
▲ Appointment. FINISHed
○ Event
● Event. Over
—☐ irrelevant—
! ☐ important
-N note
👁 Research
Money. Matters
! 💡 idea

-N: keep your SIGNIFIERS simple
if you CREATE. YOUR OWN.
Not. every BuLLet. needs a
SIGNIFIER!

You can create your own signifiers, but I recommend they be simple and as few in number as needed. The concept of the bullet journal is to use the absolute minimum of effort and methods to be productive.

BULLET · JOURNAL · BASIC · ELEMENTS

The · Index

The · Future Log:
· ~~Important dates:~~
    Birthdays
    Anniversaries
    Holidays

The · Monthly · Log:
· monthly plans / events at a Glance
· your calendar
· Deadlines
· Bills Due
· Miscellaneous

The · Daily · Log:
· Tasks that Day
· Notes to Yourself
· Ideas
· A record of your LIFE and
· so Much MorE

Bullets: the tasks, events and notes
you record in your BuJo. The 'stuff.'

Signifiers are the SYMBOLS that
give MEANING to your Bullets!

DECORATING YOUR BULLET JOURNAL

Check out some of the other projects in this book for ideas on how to decorate your planner pages. My BuJo has stains on it where I've used it to set my coffee cup.

My advice if you are new to the BuJo method is to learn the basics first before you explore the unlimited possibilities. Just remember, done is better than perfect.

YOU CAN DO THIS!

If you are new to the bullet journal method, it may seem overwhelming at first. The key to the BuJo is to write down everything, assign it a symbol, and then get it done! Some steps may seem redundant, but they will inform you quickly whether or not a task is actually a priority for you.

Remember, when you use the bullet journal method, you are never limited by pre-printed pages. Fill your BuJo with topics such as Goals, Notes, Programs to Watch, Daily Gratitude, etc. It's your journal, your life. It's as unique and wonderful as you are.

You can't do it wrong! Start with an inexpensive composition notebook and a pencil if you're nervous at first. With bullet journals, what you do is more important than what you have.

My BuJos have become a tale of my life, with pages of diagrams, doodles, plans, and story lines. A BuJo is where a planner meets a journal and combines the functions and best qualities of both. By using the bullet journal system, you have not only a planner, but a keepsake of your unique life.

WHAT TO DO WITH THOSE BLANK UNDATED PAGES

Write lists! (The BuJo term for these is "Collections.")

Favorite Quotes

Programs to Watch

Books to Read

Places to Visit

Places I've Visited

Financial Goals

Fitness Goals

Things to Do

Things to Buy

Inventories

. . . and so much more.

ABOUT THE CONTRIBUTOR

THERESA HALL is an artist, writer, and instructor who has consistently used the bullet journal method of planning for more than ten years. She recently taught bullet journal workshops at PlannerCon San Francisco 2017 and at the first PlannerCon Europe, in Brussels, Belgium, in October 2017.

How long have you been bullet journaling and what got you started?

I've been bullet journaling for as long as I've consistently carried a planner, which is over ten years. I've always kept to-do lists in my planner and created symbols for the items on my lists. I use a simple and clean method of planning and found Ryder Carroll's Bullet Journaling on the Internet.

Do you prefer to use your BuJo for long-term or short-term goals?

I use my bullet journal for long-term goals and planning. My goals consist of trying to organize my busy life and travel, since my husband lives and works in Los Angeles and I'm based in Colorado Springs, Colorado.

Any words of advice for someone who's just getting started and feeling a bit apprehensive about mussing up their planner?

My advice to anyone getting started is to remember that a bullet journal is just a planner. You can do the BuJo method in any kind of notebook. Don't compare yours to anyone else's. Write in pencil in a composition tablet if you're apprehensive at first. Most of all, remember done is better than perfect.

HOW to MAKE your NOTES STAND out

1. Make one word in your notes **LARGER** than others with block outline letters.

2. Use a label maker to write the note or a `PORTION` of the note.

3. Stick down a post-it note or sticker & write on that!

4. Draw doodles indicative of the ↑ 🎂 note's 💩 content. ⭐ ♥

5. Block off the note with washi tape.

6. Color in an area with a water-based marker, then use a water brush to lightly move the ink around. Let dry, then write over it.

7. Assign colors to your notes to indicate importance.

8. Use shapes/colors to accent certain words.

9. Box your note in with a scribble or other doodles such as lines, circles, etc, around it.

10. Vary your writing between cursive and print.

11. Use a light-colored marker to doodle a pattern, then write the note over it in black ink.

12. Start the note with the first word written sideways or rotated and large.

Making Your Notes Stand Out

Ideas

1. Write one word in your notes larger than others with block outline letters. Add shadow lines and/or color.

2. Use a label maker to write the note or a portion of the note. Bright tape colors will make these words pop.

3. Stick down a Post-It Note or plain sticker for writing on.

4. Doodle the note instead of writing, or add doodles to it.

5. Place Washi tape around the note.

6. Create a spot of color by swirling a water-based marker in a small drop of water on the page. Write over it once it's dry.

7. Color your notes to show importance.

8. Add shapes and colors to a word to make it stand out.

9. Mark a note with doodles like lines and circles around it.

10. Change up writing with both script and regular letters.

11. Create a pattern with doodles, then letter the note over it in a darker color.

12. Make the first word of the note sideways or large to differentiate the note.

SUPPLIES NEEDED:

LABEL MAKER (SUCH AS DYMO)

PENS (I USE SAKURA MICRONS)

MARKERS (I USE TOMBOW MARKERS OR WATER-SOLUBLE MARKERS)

WASHI TAPE

SCISSORS

BLANK STICKERS OR STICKY NOTES (SUCH AS POST-IT NOTES)

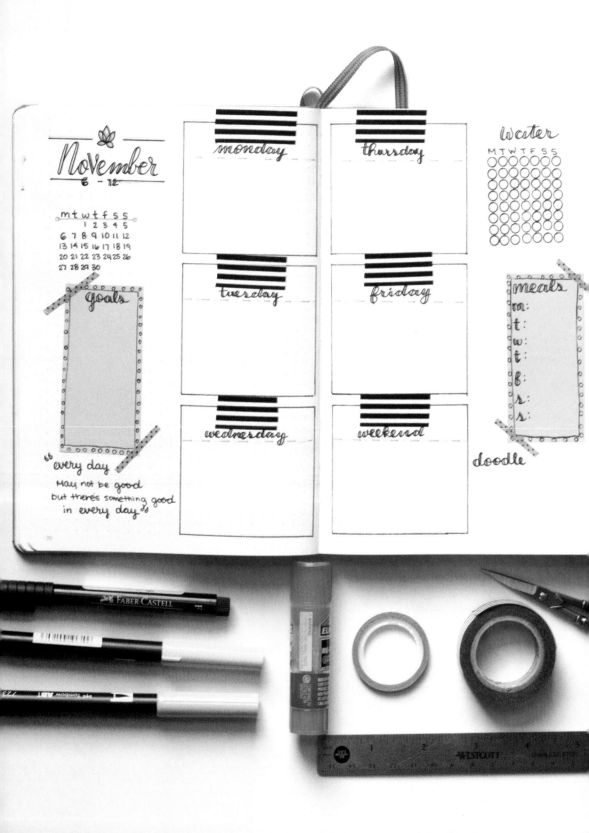

Weekly Bullet Journal Spread

Instructions

Open your journal to a blank two-page spread. Using your fine-point black pen and ruler and starting at the spine, draw a box that is ½ the width of the page and ⅓ the height of the page. Draw two more identical boxes directly below the first box, leaving a small horizontal gap between each box. Mirror these boxes on the adjacent page. You should have six identical boxes in total.

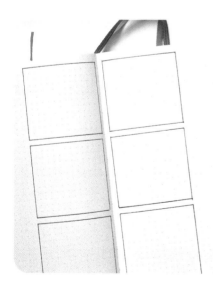

SUPPLIES NEEDED:

GRID OR DOT GRID A5 JOURNAL

FINE-POINT BLACK PEN (I USED A .3 NIB, BUT ANY FINE-POINT SIZE WILL WORK)

2 FINE-TIP MARKERS OF YOUR COLOR CHOICE (I USED PASTEL PINK AND PALE BLUE)

RULER

SMALL CIRCLE STENCIL (I USED THE HOLE ON THE END OF MY RULER)

4 INCHES THIN WASHI TAPE OF YOUR CHOICE

6 INCHES REGULAR WIDTH (15MM) WASHI TAPE OF YOUR CHOICE

GLUE STICK

SCISSORS

1 In the upper left corner, write the current month and date span with your black pen. Use your pen and markers to add some doodles around the header for decoration.

3 Just below the header, count out seven boxes from the outer edge of the page. Use your pen to draw a mini calendar of the current month, labeling the days of the week in the top row. Then use one of your markers to highlight the week the spread will be used for.

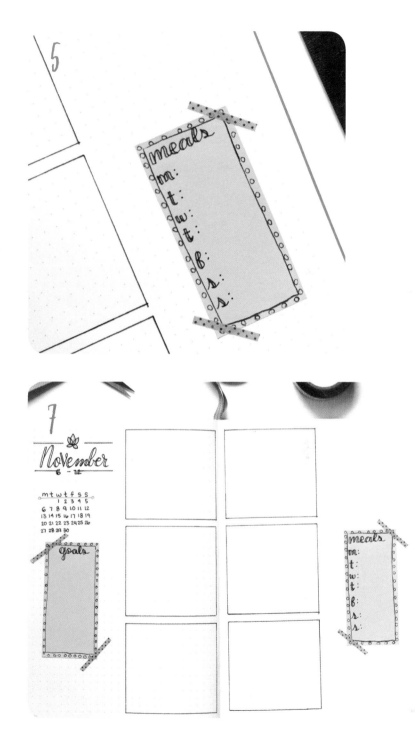

4 Use a pair of scissors to cut two rectangles out of your paper. Be sure that the rectangles will fit within the remaining column of your page, leaving some room at the bottom. For my A5 size notebook, this piece of paper measured 1 ½ x 3 inches.

5 Glue the piece of paper into your journal, right under the mini calendar. Use your black pen to create a decorative border on the pieces of paper.

6 Then, grab your thin washi tape and tear off two 1-inch pieces. Diagonally stick the tape over the corners of the paper you just added.

7 Repeat Step 5 with the remaining piece of paper on the opposite page. Then, use your fine-tip black pen to label the pieces of paper "Goals" and "Meals" or whatever other categories will help you organize your week. In the Meals box, vertically

write the letters of the days of the week on the left side.

8 In the bottom left corner, write an inspiring quote with your black pen.

9 Moving onto the opposite page, grab your fine-tip black pen and write "Water" at the top of the open column of the page. In the row below that, write the letters of the days of the week. For example, if your week starts on Monday, you would write, "M T W T F S S." One letter per box.

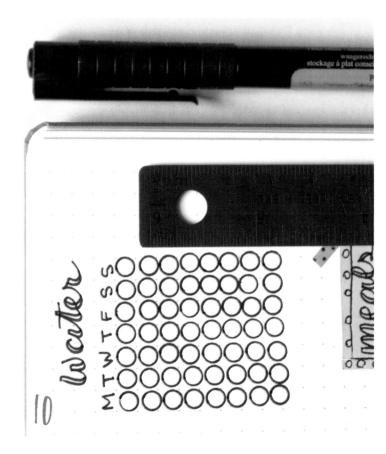

10 Then, use your small circle stencil to draw eight circles under each of the days of the week. You should have a total of fifty-six circles in a grid pattern when you are done.

11 Leave the bottom right corner of the right-hand page for doodles. You can use your black fine-tip pen to write the word "doodle" below the "Meals" box so that you remember what the space is for.

12 Go back to your six large boxes. Grab your thicker washi tape and tear off six 1-inch pieces. Place one piece along the top of each box, centering it.

13 Next, use your black pen to write the days of the week at the top of each box. Because there are only six boxes, it's best to label them "Monday," "Tuesday," "Wednesday," "Thursday," "Friday," and "Weekend."

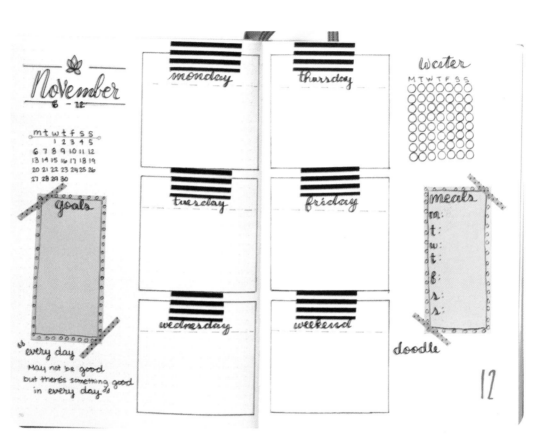

Then, use your markers and ruler to draw horizontal dashed lines under the headers of the days of the week in each box. I alternated between the two markers, creating one dash in pink and then one in blue.

Of course, all of this is customizable. That's the fun of a planner—it's tailored exactly to you and your needs. Make it work for you!

ABOUT THE CONTRIBUTOR

ERIN NICHOLS is a full-time creative blogger at thepetiteplanner.com, mom of two girls, and soon-to-be wife. She and her family live in beautiful Bozeman, Montana, with their two dogs. Erin has always had a passion for putting pen to paper, but it wasn't until January 2017 that she started sharing her passion and teaching others how to embrace their creative side. Since then, she has established a popular journaling blog, been featured in three books, and created her own creative journaling e-course. Aside from being a stationery addict and doodlebug, Erin is extremely involved in health and fitness. She regularly runs in local races, and spends her summers hiking to new destinations in the Northwest.

You clearly have a talent for creating beautiful bullet journals. What is it about this format that you connect with so deeply?
I love the flexibility of the bullet journal system. It allows me to be as creative or as simple as I want. Some weeks I spend a couple of hours on a single spread, and other weeks I quickly jot down to-do lists and upcoming events. There are no expectations, and it makes the system a lot less intimidating than a traditional planner.

What do you find more satisfying when using a BuJo: planning items or crossing them off the list once they've been accomplished? How does that play into how you use BuJos for your personal life?
I definitely lean more toward crossing them off my list. It makes me feel accomplished, and I get to visualize how productive I was for the day. I use my BuJo for my personal life every day. I'll write down all my tasks, even those that are really small, so that at the end of the day I have stuff to cross off. It's kind of like tricking your brain. Even crossing off simple tasks like "put the dishes away" or "bathe the kids" makes me feel motivated to do more and be more productive.

Many of your journals center on self-care. How have you been able to use BuJo to incorporate that into your daily life?
Mainly, I include self-care in my habit tracker. That way, I am reminded to take those

actions every day. I have also created lists of actions that relate to self-care, so when I need some Me Time, I can flip to the page and get an idea of things I can do. It certainly makes it easier, because seeing it every day makes me be more conscious about what I'm doing and what I should be doing.

Does it help you envision the grander picture while also keeping up with the minute details and small tasks of everyday life?

Absolutely. I have pages and pages dedicated to my quarterly and annual goals. I also use reflection pages to look back and see how far I have come. But my weekly logs help me keep track of the small tasks and actions that add up to big results eventually.

How does BuJo help you realize your goals and dreams? What about the form helps you to stay grounded while still allowing you to dream? Can—and should—it do both?

It gives me the space to dream freely and keep track of those hopes and dreams. I can look back at last year's journal and see what goals I had set for myself in comparison to the current year. Then I can compare and see if I'm still striving for the same thing, or if my intentions have shifted. Keeping everything written down helps me stay grounded. It's not like a dream or goal that's just in your head and can be changed at any moment. You have to look at those goals regularly, and by doing that, you are forcing yourself to not give up or minimize your goals. However, the open format and the flexibility allow me to add in new entries, think on paper, and brainstorm my dreams. So, yes, the system allows both and I think that's part of what makes it so effective and enticing.

Making lists is an essential part of bullet journaling. What is it about making lists that you appreciate the most?

There are so many things I love about making lists. But if I have to choose one thing, it's that having tasks written down ensures they won't be forgotten. Even if I don't accomplish something, I can look back a few days, see that I had a specific task I needed to do, and then migrate it to the current day and do it then. It makes me feel very organized, which in turn brings me a lot of peace knowing that I'm not forgetting anything.

RE-USE in YOUR PLANNER

Vintage Photos:
COPY ON COLOR COPIER FOR BEST RESULTS. CUT PHOTOS OUT IN FULL OR ONLY CUT PEOPLE OR subjects and paste down on pages.

Labels:
some will PEEL off EASILY, WHILE others MAY REQUIRE HOT water and patience.

← RECEIPTS and ticket stubs

★ PAPER from FORTUNE COOKIES

STAMPS AND POSTAGE

RIBBON

TORN BITS: THESE INCLUDE PIECES of NOTES, VINTAGE ledger PAGES GRAPH PAPER, COPIES OF ART YOU'VE made, CANDY WRAPPERS...

You've ← **RAD**

Skill Level: *Beginner* • Budget: *$10*
Time: *Varies*
Contributor: *Dawn DeVries Sokol*

Planning with Recycled Art

Adding odd pieces to your planner will personalize your pages. I collect all kinds of ephemera to collage onto my journal pages, and you can do the same in your planner. Look out for interesting bits whenever you're out.

VINTAGE PHOTOS: Copy the photos on a color copier, even if they are black and white, to preserve detail. Cut them out in full, or cut people or subjects out of photos, then paste down. Outline lightly with an oil pastel crayon or graphite pencil. Blend with your fingertip for a shadow effect.

LABELS: Some labels will peel easily off glass, while others may require some hot water and patience. Soak them in hot water for about 5–10 minutes, then peel. Make sure to SLOWLY pull the label from the glass to avoid tearing.

RECEIPT STUBS AND TICKETS: Stubs and tickets are easy to stash. Keep an envelope or pouch for just this purpose.

WORDS FROM PRINTED MATERIALS: You can use bits from magazines, old books, ledgers, copies of art you've made, graph paper, scrapbook paper, candy wrappers, paper from fortune cookies—just about anything that lays flat.

RIBBON: Keep a jar of ribbons. When in a store that carries them, buy a yard of whatever catches your eye.

STAMPS/POSTAGE: If you receive mail from overseas, tear out the postmarks and stamps. Keep them for later use.

SUPPLIES NEEDED:

GEL MEDIUM AND/OR GLUE STICK (I ALSO LIKE TO USE TOMBOW MONO ADHESIVE)

SCISSORS

PENS/MARKERS

GRAPHITE WATER BLENDABLE PENCIL (SUCH AS STABILO PENCIL) OR OIL PASTEL CRAYONS

Skill Level: *Beginner* • Budget: *$5*
Time: *5-15 minutes*
Contributor: *Job Gavello*

The Way of Washi

Instructions

PROJECT A: WASHI TAPE SAVE THE DATES

You can block off several days in your planner by using thin washi tape to plan multiday events. This is great for vacations or if a friend comes to visit. Start by laying down your washi tape on the day you want to highlight, and then cover each following day with tape. Stop adhering the washi tape once you've reached the last day you want to highlight.

SUPPLIES NEEDED:

PLANNER

SCISSORS

WASHI TAPES

PENS

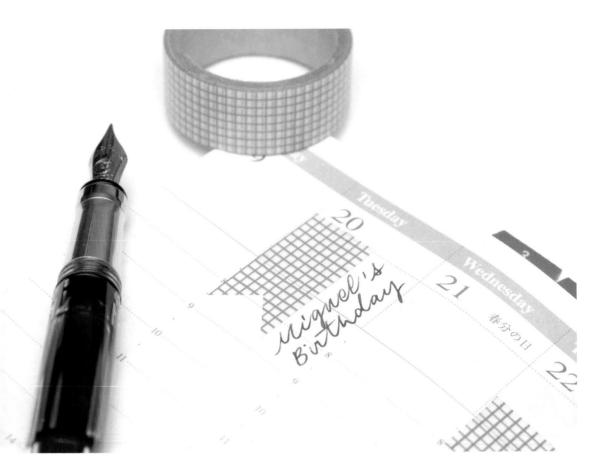

PROJECT B: WASHI TAPE FLAGS

You can use washi tape to block off a period of time in your planner by creating a washi tape flag that spans from the beginning of the time of your event to the end. For example, you might use a flag to designate an event from 12–2 p.m.

1 Cut a piece of washi tape and fold it in half (decorative side to decorative side).

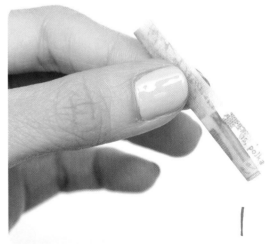

3

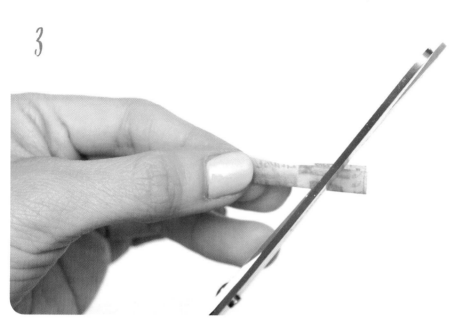

4

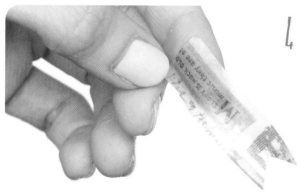

3 Use your scissors to cut the washi tape on a 45-degree angle (preferably near one of the edges of the tape so you don't waste any).

4 Trim the other end of the washi tape (non-flag end) to the proper length.

5 Adhere the tape to your planner and add any appropriate title near the washi tape flag.

5

PROJECT C: WASHI TAPE TAB

1 You can highlight or bookmark a certain page in your planner by creating a washi tape flag tab. Start by cutting a piece of washi tape that's roughly 2 inches long and adhere about ½ inch of the washi tape to the edge of the planner page.

2 Measure about ½ inch (or however tall you want your tab) from the edge of the page and fold the washi tape on itself. This should create a washi tape tab that is equal in length on both sides of the page.

3 To turn this regular square tab into a flag tab, make two diagonal cuts on each corner of the tab to create a flag shape.

PROJECT D: STRIPED WASHI TAPE PLANNER COVER

1 Choose a few of your favorite washi tapes that you would like to use to cover a planner. If you would like a more cohesive look, pick washi tapes that are similar in color.

2 Lay the first strip of washi tape down along the edge of the cover vertically. Don't worry about any overhanging washi tape, because you will cut all of those overhanging pieces later.

3 Lay the second strip of washi tape beside the first washi tape vertically. To ensure that the existing planner cover

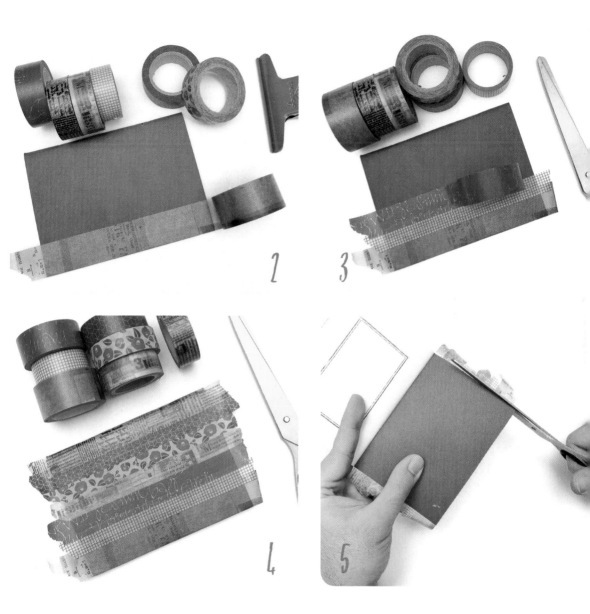

doesn't peek through, overlap the second piece of washi tape with the first so there aren't any gaps.

4 Continue steps 2 and 3 with different rolls of tape until you reach the edge of the planner.

5 Take your scissors and trim away the overhanging washi tape pieces on the top and bottom edges of the planner.

6 Repeat all steps if you would like to cover the back cover of your planner.

Wednesday	Thursday 9	Friday 10	Saturday 11	Sunday 12	November **11** 2017

MOOD TRACKER   MOOD TRACKER   MOOD TRACKER

6 to 12
45 week

To Do:
- Clean shoes
- Prepare 2nd bed room for guests
- Laundry
- Pick up cake

BUY
GROCERIES
- ☐ Apples
- ☐ Milk
- ☐ Bread

3
CANADA

Meet Migi at Cocoro & buy chicken after work

fried

chicken night!

PICK UP

DOM & CHRIS AT THE AIRPORT @ 10:00 PM

Movie night with Ashley & Deanna

CANADA

WRAP gift for Kristin & make a card!

Facetime call with Jarred, Natasha, Justine & Lourdes

happy Birthday Kristi

h b d

Dinner with Family for Aunt Kristin's Birthday!

↳ Don't forget the gift!

Oct.10 2017
M T W T F S S
            1
2 3 4 5 6 7 8
9 10 11 12 13 14 15
16 17 18 19 20 21 22
23 24 25 26 27 28 29
30 31

Nov.11
M T W T F S S
      1 2 3 4 5
6 7 8 9 10 11 12
13 14 15 16 17 18 19
20 21 22 23 24 25 26
27 28 29 30

Dec.12
M T W T F S S
        1 2 3
4 5 6 7 8 9 10
11 12 13 14 15 16 17
18 19 20 21 22 23 24
25 26 27 28 29 30 31

Jan.01 2018
M T W T F
1 2 3 4 5
8 9 10 11 12
15 16 17 18 19
22 23 24 25 26
29 30 31

Feb.02
M T W T F
      1 2
5 6 7 8 9
12 13 14 15 16
19 20 21 22 23
26 27 28

Designing Pages with Watercolor

Instructions

You can use watercolors to emphasize certain events in your planner in a fun and colorful way. I like to create small watercolor doodles that correspond to events happening during the week to add more visual interest in my planner spread.

Note: Don't use too much water while painting or your paper will warp or buckle. You will learn after a couple tries how much water to leave on your brush.

SUPPLIES NEEDED:

PLANNER
WATERCOLOR PAINTS
WATERCOLOR PAINTBRUSH
CUP OF WATER
PENS
CLIPS

1 Prepare your planner for painting by using clips or clamps to keep your planner open. This will prevent your planner from closing in on itself when you are painting in it.

2 Create a sprig by painting a leaf that's connected to a stem. Add more leaves to the stem to complete the sprig. Paint two sprigs to form a border around your planned event or a message you would like to highlight.

2A

2B

2C

3 Going on a trip or picking up someone at the airport? Paint the silhouette of a small airplane to indicate that special day. Make sure to write down the details of your event around your painted airplane.

4 Painting a small shopping cart is a great way to indicate an upcoming trip to the grocery store. If you're intimidated to paint without any guidelines, use a pencil to sketch a rough outline before you paint.

5 If you're planning a special meal, why not paint a little preview of that meal or dish in your planner? Paint a rough outline of your meal with your paints, and then add details with a fine-tip pen once the paint has dried. You can also use your brush and paints to create some basic brush lettering in your planner.

6 If you don't have any special events or meals set for a specific date, you can still jazz up empty spaces in your planner by painting a simple rose. Start by creating small dots to form the center of your rose. Create petals by painting small half-moon shapes around the small dots you have

created. Add a second layer of half-moons around the petals you initially painted. Make sure to make the petals larger with each layer to create a full rose.

7 Painting balloons is a great way to signify someone's birthday in your planner. Paint

two small circles or ovals with your water-color paints and then make sure to use a pen to draw in the strings of your balloons. Add some brush lettering around your balloons to make someone's birthday really stand out in your planner.

8 Paint circles at the top of each date in your planner. At the end of every day, draw a face that reflects your mood in the circle. By the end of the week, you'll have a completed mood tracker that can show you how you've been feeling that week.

9 Complete your planner spread by decorating it with your favorite washi tapes, stamps, and stickers. Make sure to add more details and plans to your planner with a pen in addition to your hand-painted doodles.

ABOUT THE CONTRIBUTOR

JOB GAVELLO is a Vancouver-based planner and journal artist. He primarily works with watercolors in his planner and journal because of the flowy and effortless look. You can find his photography and artwork on Instagram and YouTube with the handle @jobsjournal.

Do you find that people start conversations or are intrigued when you're using your beautiful planner in public?

People are definitely intrigued with my planner when I'm working on it in public. I think many people associate planners with organization, and when they see someone using a planner in a different or unconventional manner, people get quite interested. It's always fun doodling or working on a planner spread at a café and seeing all the shocked faces and smiles of passersby and workers.

Did you study art in school? If so, tell us about your favorite class. If not, tell us about your favorite tool or tutorial for your self-taught artistry.

I didn't attend art school (as much as I would have loved to). I'm self-taught, and I thank YouTube for that. There are so many great teachers and artists on YouTube who post tutorials that are fun and easy to follow.

You recently made a big move. Are you excited to see new planner items in the shops in Vancouver?

Having grown up in Vancouver, I never

realized all the great stationery stores at my disposal. It was only when I moved to South Korea that I came to enjoy fine stationery and paper goods. I'm excited to explore the stationery scene in Vancouver, but I definitely miss the Midori-brand translucent circle stickers that I started using when I was still living in South Korea.

Your tools and photographs have such a strong yet approachable masculinity to them. Did you study photography or are you just naturally drawn to leather goods and metal?

Ever since I was a child, I've enjoyed photography and I vividly remember having a bright red film camera. From that point on, I've been interested in documenting and photographing things I own, and I developed my own distinct style of photographing things. I love the contrast of a stark white background with the rich yet rugged look of a scuffed-up leather journal and stationery items.

DIY Elements

THESE ELEVEN PROJECTS WILL
HELP YOU MAKE YOUR PLANNER
DISTINCTIVELY YOUR OWN!

Time to get your hands dirty! In this section you'll learn how to make your planner dazzle, from carving stamps to tying tassels and knots to fancying up paper clips and bookmarks, and so much more. It's all about searching your junk drawer for good glue, hand tools, fabric, and even sequins.

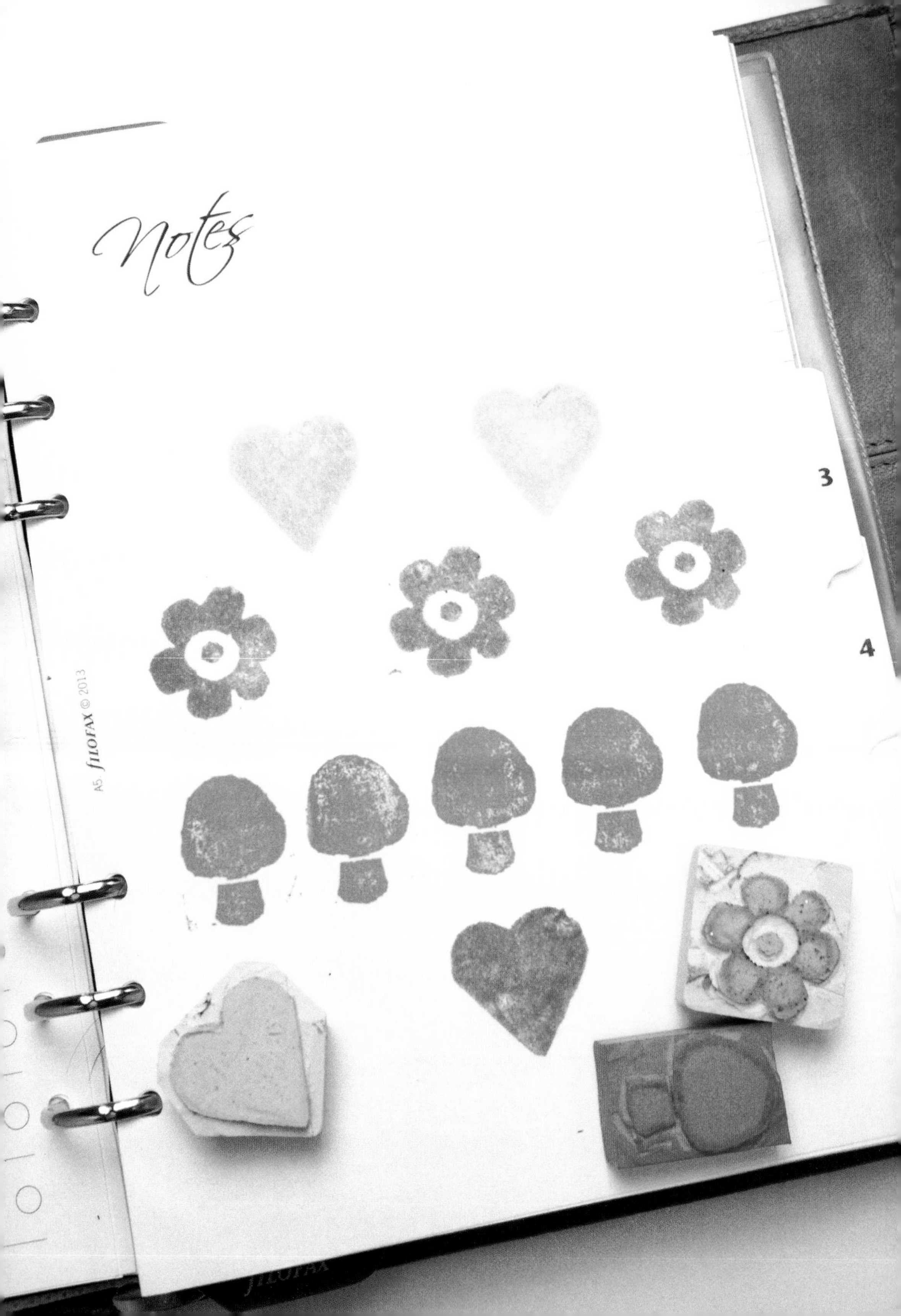

Notes

A5 FILOFAX © 2013

3

4

Skill Level: *Easy* • Budget: *$20*
Time: *2½ hours*
Contributor: *Kate Pullen*

Carving Stamps for Your Planner

Carve your own unique stamps from erasers to decorate your planner pages. When you are choosing designs for your stamps, remember that you will be working in small scale, so simple designs will not only display better, they will also be easier to carve. Just because a design is simple doesn't mean you can't have fun with it. I love to customize my stamped images further by doodling cute faces into the finished image.

Note on supplies

I used *Pink Pearl* erasers in this project; however, any eraser works well for stamp carving. You will find that different types of erasers have different qualities, so experiment and see which works best for you. If you get the stamp carving bug, check out stamp carving blocks from your local craft store or online. These are rubber blocks that are available in larger sizes.

SUPPLIES NEEDED:

DESIGN FOR STAMP

SOFT PENCIL

ERASERS

CARVING TOOL AND
  BLADES (OPTIONAL)

CRAFT KNIFE

STAMP PAD

PAPER FOR PRACTICE

Instructions

1 First draw your design on scrap paper using a soft pencil. Place the design facedown onto the eraser and rub over the back to transfer the design to the eraser. Go over any places where the design hasn't transferred well. Of course, you can draw straight onto the eraser; however, that presents fewer opportunities for correcting mistakes.

2

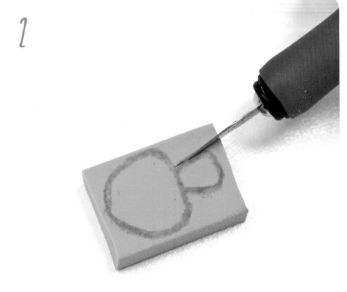

3 Start carving around your design. Use the craft knife to cut down into the eraser and then carefully slice in from the side to remove the unwanted pieces. Cut down to a depth of about ⅛" (3mm). Don't worry about being too precise with the depth. The important thing is to make sure there are no unwanted pieces that are raised high enough to leave a mark around your design.

If you have a carving tool, use a fine blade to cut around your design and use a thicker blade to cut away the rest.

1 Use the craft knife to trim away any large parts of the eraser you won't be using. This not only saves you carving away large unwanted sections, it also helps to ensure you don't get unwanted marks on the paper.

3

4 Stamp your design onto scrap paper when you have the basic shape to see how your design came out. When carving around your stamp, remember it is impossible to put back the pieces you have carved, so it is better to work by cutting small pieces at a time to avoid irreversible mistakes.

5 Continue trimming away and testing your stamp until you are happy with the results.

TIPS FOR STAMPING IN YOUR PLANNER

Look for dye-based ink pads for your planner. These are quick drying and will avoid ink smudges on the page.

Clean your stamps between use. Baby wipes are handy for cleaning ink off a stamp mid-session.

Store your stamps flat so they don't get damaged.

6 Your stamp is now ready to use in your planner. If you don't intend to use your stamp straight away, clean it with water and a little detergent. This is particularly important if you intend to use different colored inks, as the dried ink may contaminate your ink pads.

About the contributor

KATE PULLEN is a lifelong crafter. Her interest in rubber stamping and stamp carving came through the realization that stamping is such a versatile craft. She has written extensively about rubber stamping and other crafts both online and in print. Kate now lives in Spain, with her husband and several blind and deaf dogs and cats they have adopted over the years. You can find out more about Kate at her website: katepullen.com.

We're so excited to include your rubber stamp tutorial in the book. How did you get started making rubber stamps?
I have always been interested in stamping and printing. I started making my own stamps to create unique designs for projects. I began by carving shapes in potatoes and gradually moved on to other materials.

Since we asked you specifically to use a Pink Pearl eraser, given that it is widely available, do you want to tell us about another composite that you prefer?
Every type of eraser has its own unique properties and no two brands are the same to work with. This is one of the exciting things about stamp carving—people can experiment with different erasers and see what works best for them. Even a pencil eraser will be suitable for carving small stamps!

Your mushroom is just the cutest. Is there a favorite topic that you like to focus on? Animals? Plants? Teacups?
I enjoy creating rubber stamps of all types. Sometimes I like to simply carve a pattern into the eraser and see where the end design takes me. I prefer bold shapes, as they can really pop from the page when stamped using a bright-colored ink.

Your tip about using baby wipes to clean the stamps was fantastic. Any other hot stamping tips you'd like to share?
My other hot tips are to keep stamping test images as you go! This way it is easier to make adjustments as you are carving rather than at the end. Store stamps carefully, as intricate designs can get damaged easily. And my last tip is to remember that if it all goes horribly wrong, just flip the stamp over and carve on the other side.

Skill Level: *Beginner* • Budget: *$10*
Time: *5-10 minutes to create the rock; 45
minutes to bake; 24 hours for glue to fully dry*
Contributor: *Brittany Fisher*

Pet Rock Planner Charm

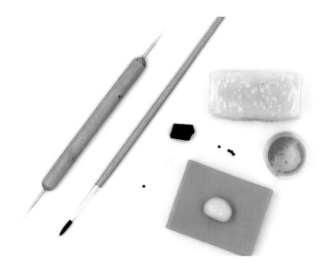

SUPPLIES NEEDED:
- *POLYMER CLAY—BLACK AND OPAL*
- *BLACK MICROBEADS (OR BLACK CLAY)*
- *SUPERGLUE*
- *POLYMER CLAY GLAZE/ GLOSS*
- *PINK CHALK PASTEL*
- *SMALL PAINTBRUSH*
- *SMALL EYE PINS*
- *SMALL DOTTING TOOL*
- *SMALL BLADE (SUCH AS AN X-ACTO KNIFE)*

These pet rock charms are more than just adorable, they can also be functional when used as a bookmark dangling from a ribbon. Whether you attach them to a lobster clasp, a ribbon, or an elastic, you'll love having this cute pet, which, as a bonus, doesn't eat much or need to be walked.

Instructions

1. Take a small amount of opal clay, about the size of a dime, and form it into a rock shape.

2. Using your dotting tool, make two small indentations into the clay directly across

from one another to create holes for the eyes.

3 Take two microbeads and put one in each indentation. Instead of microbeads, you can also use black polymer clay by rolling two small pieces into balls that fit into the indentations. Be sure to press the microbeads or clay lightly to secure them in the rock.

4 Take a very small amount of black clay and roll it out until it is thin and snake-like. Use your blade to trim off any excess clay until you are left with a short thin strip of clay. Bend the clay into a smile and gently add it to your rock using your dotting tool. Once the smile is on your rock, press it lightly to help it adhere.

5 Using your blade, scrape the pink chalk pastel until you have a small amount of chalk dust. Lightly dip your paintbrush into the dust and gently place the end of the brush on the cheeks of your rock, next to the eyes and slightly below. Continue this process until you've achieved the amount of blush you would like your rock to have.

6 Next take a small eye pin and insert it into the very top of your rock. If your eye pin is too long, you can trim it to the appropriate length using a pair of scissors or wire cutters.

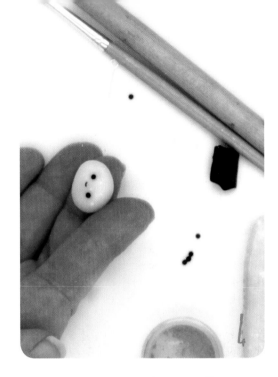

7 Bake the rock according to the clay manufacturer's directions.

8 Once your rock has cooled, use your paintbrush to gently add the polymer clay glaze/gloss to add shine to your rock and keep the blush in place.

9 Remove the eye pin from the rock. Add a small amount of superglue to the end of the eye pin and reinsert it into the top of the rock. Allow twenty four hours for the glue to fully dry.

About the contributor

Brittany Fisher is a polymer clay enthusiast, holiday junkie, self-proclaimed nerd, and lover of all things planner related. She is a crafter at heart, and besides polymer clay, she enjoys a variety of other crafts including painting, DIYs, and old-fashioned letter writing. She is a bibliophile and aims to read a minimum of fifty books this year. Brittany can usually be found in her studio working on a string of projects or with her nose in a book. She lives in Virginia.

Your pet charms are so adorable and super fun to make. Have you adapted the size to any projects that would be great for little kids' hands?

I have not specifically adapted the size of my projects for little kids' hands, but I think these pet rocks would make wonderful keepsakes or ornaments.

How did you discover the "blush" for the rocks?

A lot of failed experimenting and watching YouTube tutorials.

Other than decorating planners, what else do you accessorize with the little guys?

I've had people tell me a variety of ways they like to use their charms! Some have added them onto their purse, bookmark, necklace, and my personal favorite, a worry rock for their daughter "so that she can always have it on her and help her worries go away."

Rough estimate, how many do you think you've made so far? It seems like a project that once you get started, it becomes so much fun that you can't stop (hence our question about what else we should put them on!).

I'd estimate I've made around one hundred of these little guys!

Skill Level: *Intermediate* • Budget: *$20*
Time: *2½ hours*
Contributor: *Melissa Dufner*

No Hassle Tassel

Decorative tassels have long adorned curtains and skeleton keys, but they can be used for so much more. Instead of simply securing an overstuffed planner with an elastic (admit it, it happens), add a tassel to make it both practical and festive.

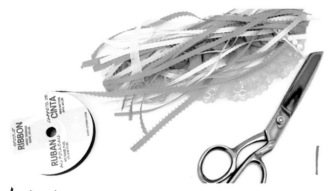

Instructions

1 Cut ribbon into 10–30 strips, each measuring 12 inches long.

2 Stack the trimmings in a flat, neat group. In the center of the bundle, tie it in the middle with the bow wire. You

Supplies Needed:

10–30 (12-inch) pieces of ribbon, strung beads, lace, or fabric. (I used teal and aqua tones for a beachy theme.)

Bow wire

Scissors

1 large split key ring

Assorted beads or charms (optional)

Head pins

Jump rings

Wire cutters

1 swivel lobster clasp

3

could also use a ribbon in a complementary color. I usually wrap it around several times to ensure that it's nice and secure. Slide the split key ring in the center.

3 Fold the bundle of trimmings in the middle using your center tie as a guide. Cut a 15-inch piece of bow wire and make a knot at the top of the tassel. Once again, I wrap it around twice for extra security.

4 Once it's nice and tight, trim off the excess bow wire and start adjusting your tassel by pulling the ribbon and the trimmings down.

4

5

6

5 Trim the tassel with scissors to give it a nice clean look. I use fabric scissors, which seem to cut through all the layers much easier.

6 I like to add bows to my tassels. When making a bow, be sure to leave plenty of bow wire, because this is how you will affix the bow to the tassel. Cut 12 to 14 inches of bow wire or ribbon that matches your tassel. Once you make the bow, thread

the wire or ribbon through the back of the bow, and then wrap the wire/ribbon around the head of the tassel and secure the bow in place.

7 To add some extra dangle, slide a jump ring into the center of the bow, and then add a combination of beads and charms.

8 To make bead dangles, string beads onto a head pin. Trim the pin with wire cutters, leaving ¼ inch of wire above the last bead to create a loop. Use round or needle-nose pliers to curve the end of the pin into a loop, and then slide it onto a jump ring to form a cluster of beads.

9 Place the completed bow on the front of the tassel, wrapping and tying the

7

bow wire around the tassel multiple times, and secure it with a knot.

9

About the contributor

MELISSA DUFNER, aka Posh Pieces, is a Texas-based artist and maker of all things for more than fifteen years. Her work is most known for its big statement pieces, planner accessories, and mixed media art. She has hosted workshops in Texas, demonstrating creative planning techniques, charm making, and mixed media techniques. Her work has been featured in local fashion shows, art shows, planner conventions, and national boutiques.

Fess up, how many planners do you own?
70+ planners, which I switch out from time to time.

When did you start making tassels for your planners?
It all began with my love for accessories. As a jewelry designer, I am always thinking of new inspiration. The planner world needed a bold statement piece, and I introduced tassels to the planner community about five years ago.

Have you branched off to making tassels for other items, like curtains and fancy skeleton keys that lead to secret rooms? (Confession, we'd want one.)
I always make it a point to say "Not just for planners." Tassels can be used to accessorize anything, from handbags, the rear view mirror in your car, key chains, cell phones, home decor, Christmas tree toppers, etc. My biggest market is the planner community, and my large Texas-sized tassels are a huge hit for handbags.

What's your favorite part of using a planner? The planning phase or reaching an end goal?
My favorite part of using a planner is decorating and accessorizing. It's another way I can express myself through creativity and document my days. The planner world is growing without a doubt, and I am happy to be a part of it!

Skill Level: *Easy* • Budget: *$5–$10*
Time: *5 minutes*
Contributor: *Heather Mann*

Colorful Ribbon Bookmarks

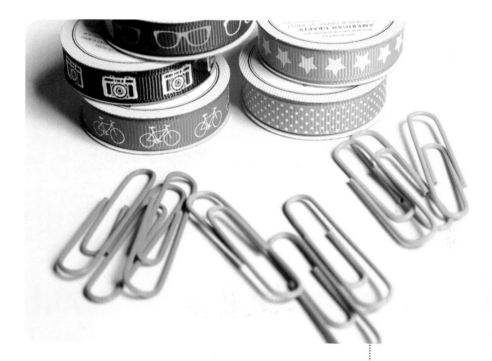

Showcase your prettiest ribbon by pairing it with paper clips to make these quick and easy ribbon bookmarks. Use these simple bookmarks to create an index in your planner, mark an important date, or to keep your place as you journal your way through the book.

SUPPLIES NEEDED:

1/4-INCH RIBBON

PAPER CLIPS

SCISSORS

GLUE (OPTIONAL)

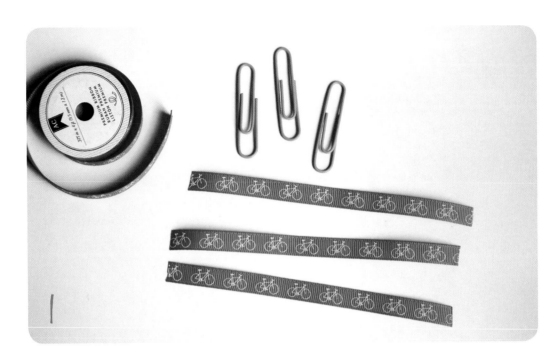

Instructions

1. Cut a piece of ribbon about 3 times the length of the paper clip.

2. Lay the middle of the piece of ribbon across the single loop side of the paper clip, with the right side facing up.

3. Wrap one end of the ribbon around the paper clip, bringing it loosely through the middle of the paper clip loop.

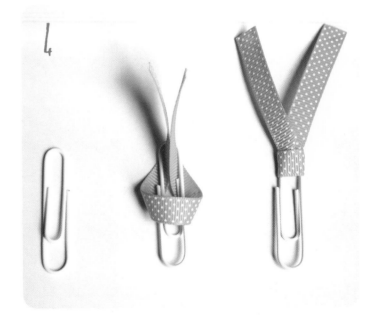

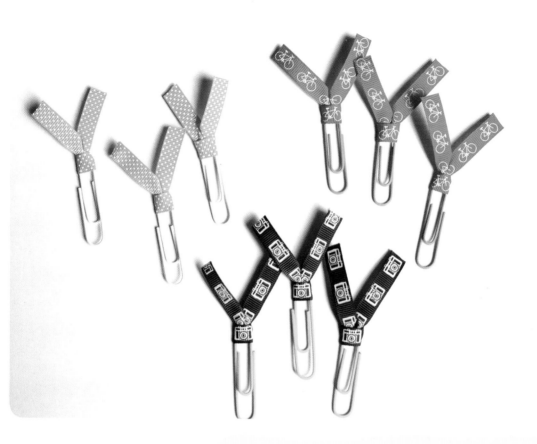

4 Repeat for the other end of the ribbon, keeping the right sides of the ribbon facing each other toward the middle of the clip.

5 Pull both of the ribbon ends to tighten the ribbon knot on the end of the paper clip.

Optional: Place a drop of glue on the ribbon while tightening to ensure the knot stays in place.

OTHER IDEAS FOR MAKING PAPER CLIP BOOKMARKS

Use washi tape folded around the edge of a paper clip to create an instant flag bookmark for your planner.

Use two pieces of ribbon for an extra fancy paper clip bookmark.

Rip strips of fabric, or use lace to create quaint, handmade ribbon bookmarks.

Skill Level: *Easy* • Budget: *$20*
Time: *30 minutes*
Contributor: *Heather Mann*

Making Decorative Tape

Make your own decorative tape (similar to washi tape) to use in your planner as dividers, decorative accents, or to make tabs for the edges of your planner for easy organization. Use any pretty printed tissue paper to create custom tape, or get creative by using gift wrap or paper you've printed with your own designs. Tissue paper is inherently thin, making it more flexible. Thicker paper may be problematic, but the results could also be fun, so don't shy away from trying.

What makes this tape different from washi tape? Washi tape fanatics will be quick to point out that authentic washi tape is made only from washi paper (a specialty paper made from plants native to Japan), which is transparent and repositionable.

Note: If you already have a paper trimmer on hand, you'll only have to spend a few dollars on the other supplies in the list. I found all my supplies at the dollar store! If you can't find freezer paper (usually in the paper products aisle

SUPPLIES NEEDED:

- *1/2-INCH DOUBLE-SIDED TAPE*
- *PRINTED TISSUE PAPER*
- *FREEZER PAPER OR WAX PAPER*
- *PAPER TRIMMER*
- *CARDBOARD ROLL OR TAPE DISPENSER (OPTIONAL)*

at your local grocery store), wax paper will work just as well.

Instructions

1   Cut a piece of freezer paper to slightly smaller dimensions than your paper trimmer. Make sure to trim the ripped edges of the paper so they are straight. This will help with cutting strips of your new tape later.

2   Lay the freezer paper shiny-side up on your work table. The waxed surface of the paper

TIPS FOR USING DECORATIVE TAPE IN YOUR PLANNER

Use decorative tape to create borders, boxes, and dividers in your planner.

Fold tape over the edge of journal pages to create indexes or for a decorative effect.

Use a piece of tape to create a quick tab on the edge of a page.

Fold a piece of tape in half lengthwise and snip diagonally to create an instant banner.

3A

3B

will allow the tape to be removed later when you want to use it in your journal. Carefully place a strip of double-sided tape against the straight edge of the freezer paper, pulling the tape tight. Place a couple more strips of tape next to the first piece. The strips of tape should be placed next to each other, but a little overlap is fine.

3 Place a piece of tissue paper over the strips of tape and rub the paper onto the tape with your fingers.

4 Turn the paper tissue-side down and place it on the paper trimmer. Use the ruler guide to cut 1/2-inch strips.

5 Store the strips of tape in an envelope inside your journal or roll them around a cardboard tube. Attach the end of a piece of decorative tape to the tube with a small bit of double-sided tape, and then wrap around the tube.

6 To use the tape, peel the tape from the freezer paper backing and adhere to your journal pages. Trim to fit.

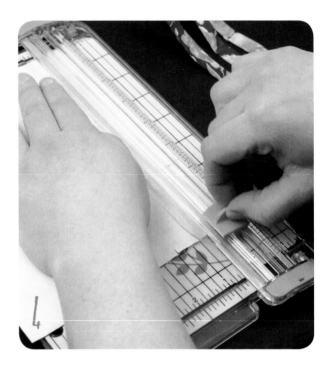

ABOUT THE CONTRIBUTOR

HEATHER MANN is the founder of DollarStoreCrafts.com, which specializes in transforming inexpensive materials into stylish and simple craft projects. She has appeared on *The Martha Stewart Show*, and in *Reader's Digest* and *The New York Times*. She shares failed craft projects on her website CraftFail.com.

Do you have a favorite type of paper for this project? Thin? Thick? Vintage wrapping paper? Tissue?

My favorite kind of tissue paper for this project is any kind that has a smaller, repeating pattern (so that the pattern translates well when trimmed into narrow strips). If you want a translucent tape, tissue paper is definitely your choice.

Any type of paper that you're definitely not a fan of for this project because it's difficult to work with?

I would encourage you to try any kind of paper that you like, just to see how it goes. That said, I would stay away from any super-thick and textured paper (like a heavy mulberry paper) because the extreme texture might not stick well to the tape.

Fun papers to try out: old maps, book pages, thin gift wrap, comic book pages, newspaper, or the yellow pages.

That tape dispenser (page 84) is adorable! Where did you pick it up?

I got it in the dollar spot at Target. You must check the dollar spot every time in case of cute stationery supplies!

We're desperate to give this a try using Liberty of London fabric from our stash of scraps. Any suggestions?

You can use the same technique shown here to make fabric tape, but instead of a paper trimmer, use a fabric rotary cutter and self-healing mat to cut the strips.

Skill Level: *Beginner–Advanced* • Budget: *$4*
Time: *1 hour*
Contributor: *Inga Breiholz*

Shake It Up Page Divider

Give your organizer a personal note with these colorful homemade page dividers.

These glittery pages will greet you when you open your planner and make you look forward to your weekly planning.

Instructions

1 Cut the transparency film according to the size of your organizer. You can simply use a page from your organizer as a guide. You will need two parts (front and back). The best result is achieved when using a cutter and a cutting mat.

2 Position the two fitted parts exactly on top of each other.

Tip: Hold the two parts in place with some adhesive tape so they won't shift while sewing later on. After sewing, the tape can easily be removed. Be mindful of cleaning or replacing the needle afterward because the tape will leave residue.

Supplies Needed:

Transparency film (the stronger/thicker the quality, the easier the sewing is going to be)

Glitter, beads, sequins, confetti, etc.

Colored cardboard, map, picture, or photograph (optional)

Sewing machine

Thread

Cutter

Cutting mat

Scissors

Puncher

3 Seam up your film on three sides. One of the long sides (the one that later on will have the binder holes) has to be sewn with a distance of ½ inch to the edge. Sew the remaining sides as close to the edges as possible. Leave one of the short sides open for now so that you can fill the divider.

For sewing the film, I recommend a zigzag stich.

5 Sew up the remaining open side of your divider.

6 Now the divider has to be punched. Line up the holes exactly with the rings on your organizer's mechanism. I recommend using a hole puncher.

See the photo below for additional inspiration.

4 Now you can decorate your divider as you desire. Use colorful paper, a lovely photo, a motivating phrase, or simply fill your bag with glitter, little beads, sequins, or even confetti. Let your imagination run free; there are no limits. Just bear in mind that all items used should be relatively flat so that later on your divider does not expand your organizer too much.

ABOUT THE CONTRIBUTOR

INGA BREIHOLZ teaches art and crafting projects to children and youths in northern Germany. Privately she loves to craft, paint, photograph, and sew. Since 2016 she's had an online shop (de.dawanda.com/shop/zimtzebra) where she offers her own designed and manufactured decorative papers, as well as dividers and filler papers for ring binders.

You can find her online at zimtzebra.blogspot.de and on Instagram: @z.mtzebra

We're so excited to have contributors from outside of the USA. Is there a big planner community in Germany?
Yes, there is a steadily growing community in Germany. Most are using Filofax, but the bullet journal is also becoming more popular.

Your dividers have such wonderful items floating around in them. Do you routinely hunt for items that are flat and can move freely or do you prefer the visual aspect of static items like maps and pictures?
The hunt is on all the time. I keep my eyes open for single items as well as static ones and I very much like to combine those two aspects. You often find them in places where you don't expect them to be. Every-day items can be lovely, as well as vintage style items such as scraps of paper with old handwriting or illustrations.

Any fun anecdotes about sewing on plastic that you'd like to share?
When sewing on plastic my sewing machine is always highly motivated, so I can hardly keep her in rein and the presser foot always tries to overtake the thread.

Do you enjoy making the dividers thematic by color or by category?
For my shop I like to make individualized shakers. Especially for people who have the travel bug, I offer to make dividers with a piece of map of a place they tell me about. And depending on their wishes, I combine small items and colors that fit the theme. For myself I create dividers that fit the current color scheme of my planner or the seasons.

What is your favorite element to use in the dividers?
I do love using maps, but the magic lies in the little glittery things. You have to choose them well, and in the end the combination of several items does the trick.

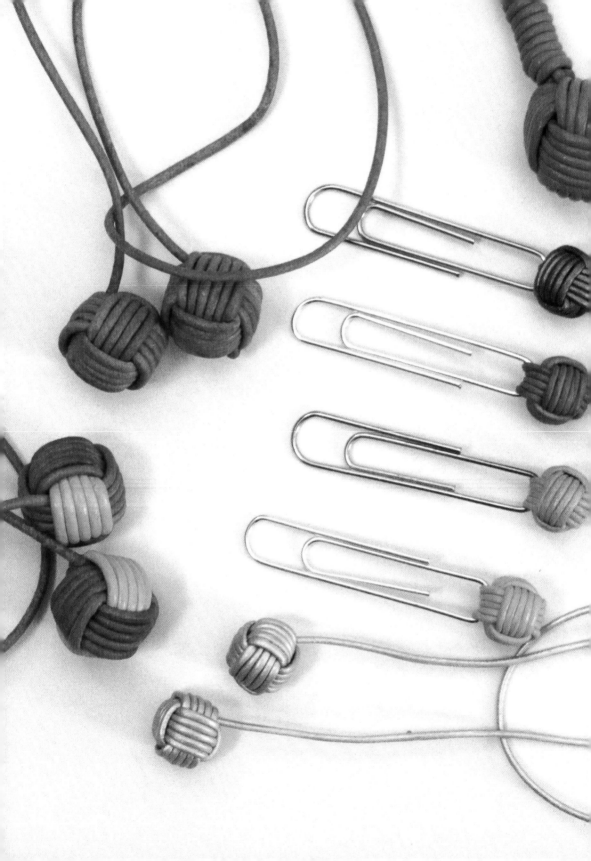

Monkey's Fist Bookmark

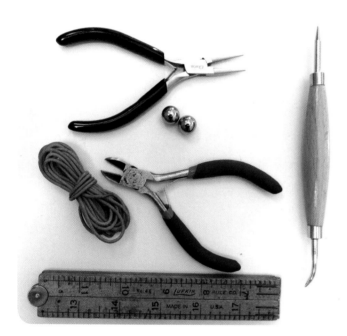

SUPPLIES NEEDED:

2MM ROUND LEATHER CORD OR PARACORD (80 INCHES FOR DOUBLE FIST KEYCHAIN/30 INCHES FOR PAPERCLIP)

2 (12MM) BALL BEARINGS (MARBLES AND BEADS CAN BE USED AS WELL)

PLIERS

SCISSORS OR CUTTER TOOL

AWL (OPTIONAL)

RULER

The monkey's fist bookmark can be used in anything, from your current novel of choice to your planner, journal, or your scriptures.

Instructions

Cut your leather cord to desired length. The length of cord needed will depend on the size of the bearings or marbles you use, as well as the thickness of the leather

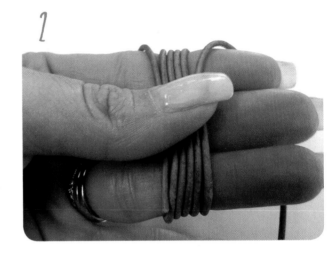

cord and the desired length of the bookmark. For this example, I am using 2mm leather cord and 12mm ball bearings to make a bookmark that fits an A5 journal or planner. An A5 planner is 8 ¼ inches tall, so you'll need roughly 80 inches of cord, which is 30 inches per ball and then 18 ½ inches between the two fists (double the height of the planner plus a few inches).

Caveat: The weight, thickness, and type of cord you use will impact the length you'll need for other monkey's fist projects. Using the 2mm cord specified in this project, you'll need 30 inches for a single monkey's fist topper for a paper clip.

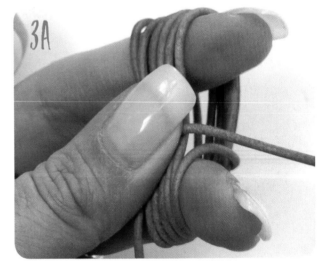

With all of this in mind, I have cut the leather 6 feet 8 inches long, providing me with a little more than an inch of cord left over.

1 Once you have cut the cord to your desired length, place your three fingers together —the fore, middle, and ring

fingers—and wrap the leather cord around them five times, keeping the end of the leather cord in place with your thumb. The amount of times you wrap the leather will depend on the thickness of the cord and the size of your ball bearing.

3 Remove your forefinger from the wrap and then begin to wrap the leather horizontally around your first vertical wrap. You must keep the number of times you wrap your leather consistent. My second round of wrapping the cord will be five times because my first round of wrapping it was five times.

4 Insert your ball bearing in the hollow space provided after the vertical and horizontal rounds of wraps are complete.

5 Complete another round of five wraps, this time vertically around the horizontal wrap completed in Step 3.

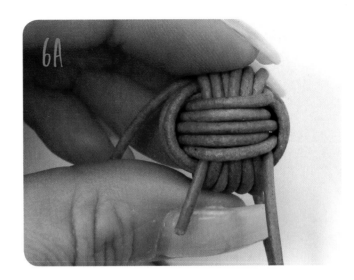

6A

6 Tuck the beginning of the cord held down by your thumb into the center of the knot to hide it. Begin pulling the cord strand by strand as you wrap it until you have it as snug as you want it. I use an awl to help with the threading of the cord through the knot, as it can sometimes be hard to get a grip with your fingers.

6B

7 Now move an inch or two down the leather cord from the completed first knot and repeat Steps 2 through 6 (but don't tuck the cord into the knot).

8 You will have a length of cord dangling. Thread the knot in the opposite direction, shortening the length of cord dangling and thereby increasing the length of cord between the two knots to the desired length of your bookmark.

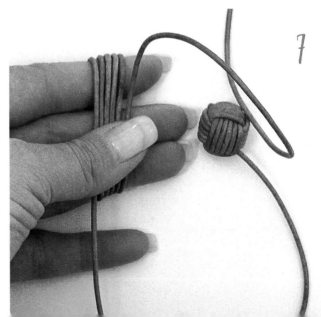

7

A SAILOR'S KNOT

The monkey's fist is an ancient nautical knot used by sailors and mariners. The knot was used as a weighted fob to propel a ship's tie-down lines to a dock. It was also used as a way to bring two neighboring ships together. In addition, it was used in the event of someone falling overboard. Back in the day, ships relied entirely on wind to propel them forward, so they were unable to turn around to retrieve any unfortunate souls who fell overboard. Even if a rope was thrown over for the person to grab, the person's hands were likely numb because of the frigidity of the water, making it difficult to grip the rope, so it would slide through their fingers. Having a monkey's fist knot gave the person something solid to grasp and hold on to, thereby allowing them to be pulled back to the ship. The monkey's fist symbolizes that lifeline/lifesaver connection to a friend, something to grasp and hold on to when we feel like we're drowning. For this reason, they make wonderful gifts to loved ones.

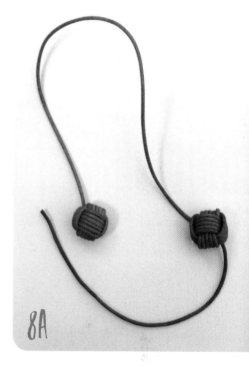

8A

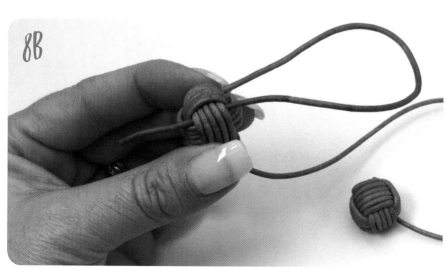

8B

9 Cut the excess cord and tuck in under the cord wrapped around the bearing to hide it.

10 In addition to bookmarks, you can create a monkey's fist topper for paper clips. Follow Steps 1 through 6. After you tuck in both ends, slide a paper clip under one of the wraps.

9B

9A

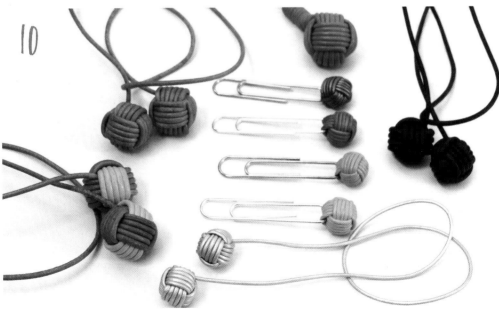

10

ABOUT THE CONTRIBUTOR

BABETTE KOPROWSKI is an accountant by day and an aspiring artist by night. She loves all things stationery related, most especially fountain pens and journals. She can be found on Instagram @babette.marie, as well as her YouTube channel and shop, Not Just Knots. She is also the mom of two grown boys, wife to an amazing hubby, and a fur mommy to one adorable Cocker Spaniel.

We love your knots! Can you tell us why it's called a Monkey's Fist? We totally thought it was called a Nautical Ball until we started working on this book.
It's called a Monkey's Fist because it resembles a monkey's closed fist or like a monkey is grasping something and it won't come loose.

Have you made any really big fists with rope? We admit, it's now on our list of post-book activities to attempt.
I have made door stoppers using a large softball.

Like knitting, do you find yourself carrying around your supplies in your purse and whipping out your stash when you're waiting somewhere?
I take it with me only when I know I will have a wait—the doctor's office, as an example—but for the most part I only make them at home. I have a whole desk set up to make them, and I schedule in time to make them daily.

Other than planners, what else do you routinely decorate with the fists? We can't wait to adapt this project and make Christmas tree ornaments with our family!
I've made Christmas ornaments for friends, but I used a golf ball for those. You could also use a Styrofoam ball for something lightweight. I have made lariat necklaces as well as bracelets and key chains, which you can see on my site. I have seen other people make place card holders with Monkey's Fists, and even curtain ties and garlands.

Skill Level: *Beginner* • Budget: *$35*
Time: *1 hour*
Contributor: *Natalie Craver*

Mum's the Word Paper Clip Topper

SUPPLIES NEEDED:

*ROLLED FLOWER AND LEAF
   TEMPLATE (ON PAGE 106)*

*2 (8 X 12-INCH) SHEETS
   WOOL FELT (1 FOR
   FLOWER AND 1 FOR
   LEAVES)*

FREEZER PAPER

FINE-TIP MARKER

CLOTHES IRON

FABRIC SCISSORS

1 CM FELT BALL

MINI HOT GLUE GUN

GLUE STICKS

1 STANDARD PAPER CLIP

Instructions

1 Cut the freezer paper to match the size of the two felt sheets. Trace the Rolled Flower and Leaf Template (on page 106) onto freezer paper using a fine-tip marker. Using the clothes iron on a warm setting (no steam), iron the freezer paper to the wool felt, waxy side down. Be sure to press lightly. Lay aside to cool.

2 Using fabric scissors, cut the petals and leaves from felt by following the traced lines. Separate the wax paper from the wool by pinching the wax paper and delicately pulling away from the felt.

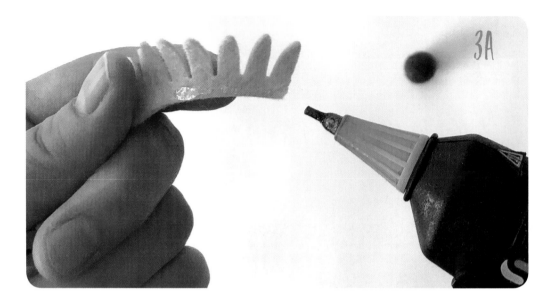

3 Begin gluing the petals to the center of the felt ball. Apply the glue directly to the strip below the petals. This piece will act as a guide for your glue gun. Wrap the petals around the felt ball, one on top of another, while continually adding glue. This will prevent the petals from unraveling. Make sure to keep the strip of felt below the petals lined up as you roll it. Repeat this for the remaining two strips of felt petals. Begin the second strip where you left off from the first strip. (I like my flowers full, so I use three strips of petals on one flower.)

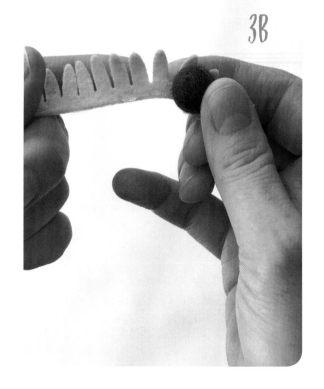

3B

4 Glue the two felt leaves together in the shape of a V.

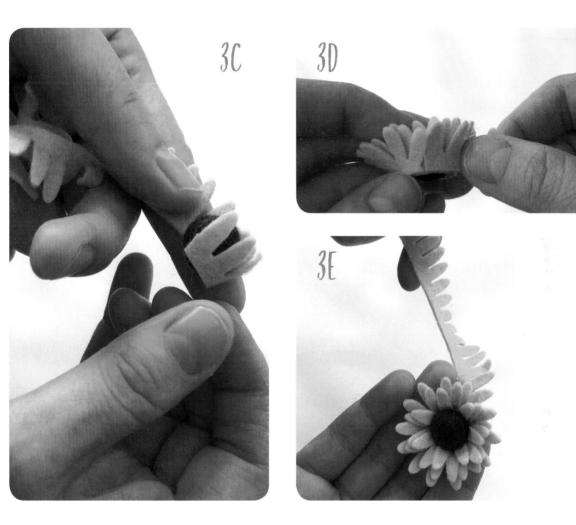

3C

3D

3E

Add a dime-size bit of glue to the bottom of the V and press in the top of the paper clip. Set aside to dry. Cut a small circle in the matching petal color and glue to the back of the flower to cover the felt ball. This will stabilize the paper clip to the flower. Add glue to the center back of the flower and press the top of the paper clip to glue. Press delicately to set in place; set aside to dry.

4

Felt Mums pattern

ABOUT THE CONTRIBUTOR

NATALIE CRAVER fell in love with the idea of having a creative outlet where she could find time to refresh and renew after the birth of her son. It was a great opportunity to connect with imagination and creativity. As a result, she became a fan of felt flower design. She started with felt flower wreaths and crowns but quickly realized the possibilities were endless. Natalie opened her Etsy shop Felt and Fauna in 2014 where she sells her felt flower creations.

When did you start making the felt toppers for paper clips? Was it a spin-off of another project?
I started making felt toppers for paper clips in the summer of 2017. I was intro-duced to the idea by a customer who adored my felt flower crowns but want-ed something smaller to accessorize her planner. It was a great opportunity and I started to roll out different collections for holidays and seasons!

Do you have a specific brand of felt that you enjoy for your projects?
I typically use a wool blend felt. The wool blend felt has quite a different texture than synthetic felt and is much easier to work with for a vast scale of projects. One of my favorite suppliers is Benzie Felt. Benzie can be found on Etsy and also on the web at www.benziedesign.com.

How about paper clips? Are you loyal to a particular type/brand of paper clip?
I generally use a jumbo-sized paper clip. There is more space available to secure a flower. I have also created bookmarks using $5/8$-inch fold over elastic. I also like to use 35mm alligator clips. Alligator clips are great for grabbing several pieces of paper at a time.

A Bounty of Bows

A handmade bow transforms an ordinary planner into a daily gift. Whether you use the bow on a paper clip or attached to an elastic, the addition will delight.

Instructions

1 To make a bow, measure and cut a piece of fabric 6 inches x 5 inches. This will make a three-inch bow. To make the bow more of a box shape, cut the fabric as a square, 6 inches x 6 inches.

2 Working on the longer side of the bow, fold the fabric in half with the wrong sides together, crease it lightly with your fingers, and then open it again. There will now be a seam running lengthwise along the middle of the piece of fabric.

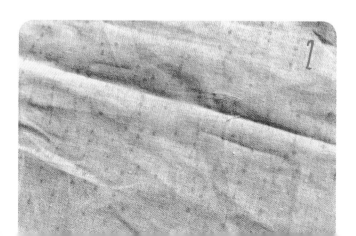

SUPPLIES NEEDED:

FABRIC FOR THE BOW

FABRIC OR RIBBON FOR THE CENTER OF THE BOW

RULER

SCISSORS

CLOTHES IRON

NEEDLE

THREAD

PLIERS (OPTIONAL)

HOT GLUE GUN

GLUE STICKS

CLASP

JUMP RING

PAPER CLIP (OPTIONAL)

3 Fold each long side of the fabric back in toward each other so they meet along the middle seam; iron.

4 Now working on the shorter side of the fabric, fold it in half, then unfold.

5 Using this new seam to guide you, fold each end in to meet at the seam, then iron. Make sure to overlap the fabric slightly in the middle. Otherwise, the needle won't pass through all layers of the fabric when sewing. You now have a flat bow.

down to thread a needle. This is particularly relevant at this stage of the bow-making process.

THE ACCORDION FOLD

7 Using the middle/center of the bow as your starting point and working lengthwise, bend the bow back so the middle gathers upward to form a peak.

6 Thread your needle and knot it at the end. I usually have a few needles already threaded to start. Once you begin working, it's often an inconvenience to put your bow

8 Folding lengthwise toward the outer edge of the bow, fold a dip followed by a peak so it looks like an accordion. The outer edge of the bow fabric should finish as a dip (imagine the bow "curled" into the back of itself all tucked away nicely). Repeat on the other side. Make sure you don't let go of your accordion. Now you've got your pre-sewn bow ready to go.

9 Take your pre-threaded needle (this is why I like to have them already thread-ed), stand the needle on your work surface with the pointy end facing up, and skewer the center of the accordion bow onto it. It's an easy way of sewing the bow and keeps it from unraveling.

10 Rock the fabric and needle back and forth to get the needle all the way through the fabric. (Sometimes I use pliers to hold on to the needle point to get a better grip of it and stop it slipping in my fingers.) Then pull the nee-dle all the way through the fabric until the knot in the end of the thread stops it.

11 Wrap the thread around the center of the bow a few times. Tie off the thread

or sew it into itself at the back of the bow, and then cut the thread. You're almost there!

12 Take a matching piece of fabric, about 1 inch x 3 inches, or some pretty matching ribbon (6mm to 9mm width). Fold it

inward to a third, then again, and iron it. If you choose to use ribbon, you can use it as is, without folding.

13 Working from the back, use your hot glue gun to glue this strip down, then bring it over to cover the front of the bow

13A

13B

13C

14

where the thread is, and around to the back again. Glue this down over the start of the strip. Cut off the excess fabric.

14 Add a jump ring and clasp for a pretty planner charm. To attach the bow to a paper clip for a page marker, glue the paper clip to the back of the bow before gluing the strip of fabric in place.

ABOUT THE CONTRIBUTOR

KATE LEMMON is a journalist and court reporter for newspapers in Brisbane, Australia. She grew up in Mackay, North Queensland. Her fondest memories are of the days she spent going to work with her dad, a veterinary surgeon. Kate has four younger sisters and together with their parents they raised orphaned possums, wallabies, and birds; kept pet ducks, chickens, and dogs; and bred Burmese cats, horses, and ostriches. She makes and sell charms, bookmarks, bows, and other accessories on her Etsy shop, Lemon Tree Prints AU. Running the Etsy shop is one of three jobs she has, but it is her biggest passion and the most rewarding. But her favorite thing in the world is being at home with her two-year-old son.

Other than making bows, what's your favorite accessory to make for your planner?
The charms. Particularly charms where I've incorporated glass lampwork beads. I love the wire wrapping technique and how they become a pendant themselves, lending their beautiful colors to the accessories I'm making.

Do you have a favorite type of fabric? Cotton? Poly? Vintage?
Cotton is the easiest to work with for bows, and my favorite color is mint blue, so when I can use those two elements I'm happy. I love vintage and floral designs, so I generally stock a lot of those styles.

The bows seem to lend themselves well to other projects like headbands, wreaths, pet collars, key chains, etc. Are you at the point where you're putting bows on everything? Because we totally want to now.
Every bow is also currently available to be purchased as a hair bow using either an alligator clip or a headband. I've also introduced planner bands (with elastic to strap around a planner) and purse charms where the bows are attached to a length of chain which wraps through a bag or purse strap. But definitely yes, if there's a demand or interest in the products you've mentioned I'm more than happy to accommodate it.

With very lightweight fabric like Liberty of London's, would a backing or interface help, or do you think it's unnecessary and would only add bulk?
It depends what I'm trying to make. For fabric bows it's a little unnecessary as the ironing and sewing process does give them structure and rigidity, and because they're a relatively small piece, they don't really need additional support.

ICEROX
CA

Hold Me Tight,
by Jean Sagendorph,
illustrated by Kim Siebold

"Siebold's enchanting
illustrations
express the enormity
of motherly love."

—Robin Preiss Glasser,
illustrator of the
FANCY NANCY series

book.com/
holdmetight

Envelopes to Be Envied

The great thing about lined envelopes is that they are thin, so you can put many different designs in your planner. And you can use a myriad of materials with this very easy (and forgiving) project. If you don't have a bone folder to make nice creases, a ruler will work just as well. You can use pretty much any paper you want: envelopes, kraft paper, bond paper, wrapping paper, maps, color photocopies, wallpaper, scrapbook paper, etc. I'm a big fan of Scotch's adhesive roller, but you can use washi tape or even just regular Scotch tape if you don't mind the look or plan to use other materials to mask it.

Once you make one of these, you'll want to make more. I'm up to forty now and swap them out when the mood strikes.

SUPPLIES NEEDED:

ADHESIVE ROLLER
SCISSORS
RULER
ENVELOPE
PAPER FOR YOUR LINER
PENCIL
HOLE PUNCH
PHOTO CORNERS
WHITE GLUE (OPTIONAL, FOR PHOTO CORNERS)

Instructions

I like my envelopes to be the same size as my other inserts so the edges don't get dented or frayed, so I use a spare

piece of paper from my planner as a guide. Using the paper, sketch out the spots for the holes with your pencil and then punch them out of your envelope. Mark the top and bottom of the envelope and cut straight across. A Fiskars paper cutter is great for the ease but unnecessary for this project.

1 Opening the envelope, you can decide how much of the liner you want to be visible. I like to leave a small amount of white around the liner to make the colors pop. Take care that your liner doesn't cover the holes. Use a roll of washi tape or another circular object to draw rounded corners on both the envelope flap and liner paper and then cut them on the line. At this point, use the ruler to put a good

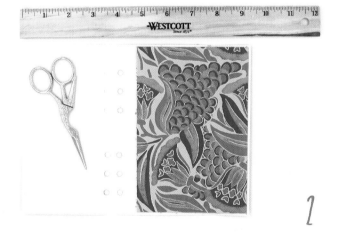

3

Decorating with washi tape and pictures you've photocopied increases the personalization.

Stamping the envelope with a title will keep you organized, such as "Receipts," "Gift Cards," "Pictures."

Because there are dozens of different sizes/types of planners, you can personalize this project to your specific needs. If you find the perfect envelope, you might not need to trim the size.

Using pinking shears or any decorative cutter will increase the fanciness.

Old maps and vintage wrapping paper are super fun to work with.

You can also apply thin paper to clear contact paper and make a plastic envelope. The fold will be problematic, so you'll want to either forgo the fold or use an adhesive Velcro dot to keep it closed.

bend in the paper where the envelope will close. Run your finger up and down the liner to make sure that you have a tight crease that folds into the crease of the envelope.

3 Turn the liner paper over and apply the adhesive tape to the smaller side of the crease (what will be the envelope flap). Carefully line up the fold of the liner with the envelope crease and move out from there with the adhesive roller to secure it to the body of the envelope.

4 Now you'll want to secure the top and bottom of the envelope so your items don't slide out. The adhesive roller is a dream for this task. If you don't have a roller, washi tape or even just Scotch tape

will work. Be sure not to put adhesive on the flap, or it will close and never open again—well, not without a big rip.

5 While photo corners are clearly not necessary, who doesn't love a little drama? If you don't have photo corners, you can easily make some by folding paper into a triangle, using a bit of adhesive, and attaching them. These glitter photo corners (from Martha Stewart) have a sticky back, so I applied a bit of leftover red paper from the envelope to the backside and dropped a bit of glue inside the corner before I inserted the envelope into the photo corner.

6 The envelope can be kept closed with a fancy paper clip, a Velcro dot, or even a button and string system if you're so inclined. I tend to let the envelope stay as it is. When the planner is closed, everything is secure due to the fold. I haven't lost anything yet.

Do you have a favorite type of paper to use as a liner for the storage envelopes?
It depends on the pattern and color. I think I'm more focused on the design than the paper itself. I love old wrapping paper patterns and wallpaper, but some of the new handmade papers are beyond dreamy. Thick papers can be problematic to fold, but you can get around that by cutting the liner into two pieces: one for the interior belly of the envelope and a separate piece for the interior flap. You could also use some washi tape in that gully to make it fancier.

Where's your favorite place to source paper?
Other than tag sales and thrift stores, where I can typically find vintage ephemera, I love Arlene's Artist Materials (www.arlenesartist.com). They have an incredible assortment of paper from both big manufacturers and local artisans. I bought the red/gold/teal paper that I used in this tutorial and made the mistake of only buying one sheet. I went back a few weeks later and couldn't find more, so I asked an employee and he helped me find it again. I think I might have scared him when I squealed and bear hugged him. I purchased many more sheets that day.

What's your favorite part about this project?
How easy it is to scale both size-wise and financially. You can use some seriously expensive materials or just items you have around the house. Also, you can personalize it by making copies of photographs and using a collage of the pics as a liner.

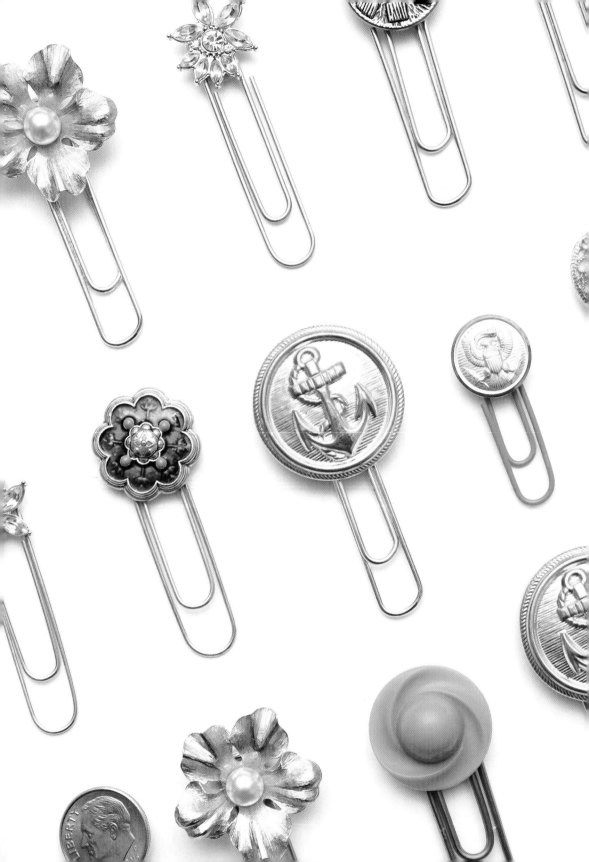

Skill Level: *Easy* • Budget: *$4*
Time: *20 minutes plus drying time*
Contributor: *Jean Sagendorph*

Fun and Fancy Paper Clips

SUPPLIES NEEDED:

FANCY ACCESSORIES (OLD EARRINGS, PINS, BUTTONS, CHARMS, ETC.)

SCISSORS

FELT

ADHESIVE (E6000 OR LOCTITE GEL)

PAPER CLIPS

CARDBOARD

EMERY BOARD (OR SANDPAPER, A DREMEL IS DREAMY TOO!)

NIPPERS OR EQUIVALENT TO SNIP THE BACKINGS OFF OF EARRINGS, BUTTONS, ETC.

SAFETY GLASSES

TOOTHPICK (OR AN EXTRA PAPER CLIP)

You can buy adorable paper clips in pretty much any retail store, but using those that you create ups the personalization factor of your planner. Even better, make them out of buttons with slogans that motivate you. I'm a sucker for clunky old costume jewelry. When I'm not making magnets

Note: My favorite adhesives for this project are E6000, which is incredibly strong and allows you to move items around for a few minutes if you need to reposition. Also, it's not drippy. Since I tend to marry metal to metal, E6000 is a dream to use.

Loctite Gel is also fantastic but does not allow you to manipulate the clip or your accessory with ease. The gel is a bit thin, so it is very easy to get it on your fingers (like with Crazy Glue) or worse, on the front of your accessory, which will likely ruin it. If you need your accessory to be in a very specific position on the paper clip, go with the E6000. Follow manufacturer's guidelines for ventilation and use.

for my fridge out of them, I'm making paper clips. My sisters (and even the photographer for this section) have been known to beg them off of me. They just have something (a certain *je ne sais quoi*, if you will) that store-bought clips don't have.

Instructions

You'll want to dry the adhesive with your paper clip facedown, so I find it easier to build a small stage out of cardboard with two different heights that accommodate the differing depths of the flat paper clip and the thicker accessory. Think of it as a massage table for your paper clip, where

the accessory is like your head resting in that odd little hole.

PIN

If you're using a pin, you'll first need to remove the backing. Next, cut small pieces of cardboard to insert in the back of the pin to build up the empty space. Glue the cardboard pieces together and to the pin so that you have a flat back for your paper clip.

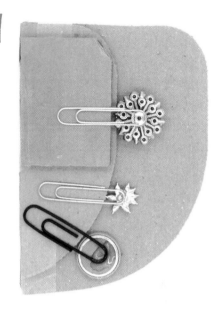

EARRINGS & BUTTONS

You'll need to remove and then file down the backing (especially if it's a vintage clip-on). Wear safety glasses because it's not uncommon for a little piece of metal to take flight. If you have a Dremel, filing down the sharp bits is easy. If not, a little more handiwork with an emery board or sandpaper will get you where you need to go. Buttons with loop backings can be a bit more problematic. If you can't get the back flush, put the button facedown on some very fluffy fabric (a few layers of flannel, for example) and gently hammer the back till it caves in on itself. Then rebuild a fake back in the same way that you would a pin (see left).

1 The paper clips should always be glued with both loops pointing down from your accessory, or it won't be able to hold anything. Decide what size/style of paper clip you want to use (I'm a fan of the bigger paper clips) and decide what direction you want the accessory to be in.

2 Cut out a small piece of felt to cover the back of the accessory (not necessary, but it gives it a bit more of a finished look). You can trim the felt down with small scissors (cuticle scissors work great) after the adhesive has dried.

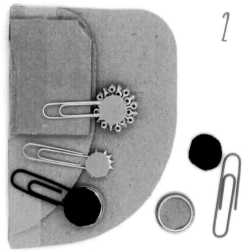

3 Place the accessory (pin, button, earring, etc.) facedown on the cardboard stage, apply a dab of adhesive, and attach the paper clip (being mindful again that both loops face away from the accessory). At this point you might want to either apply a bit more glue so that it enrobes the paper clip, or use a toothpick (or another paper clip) to move the glue around. Start small with the glue; it's easier to add more, but harder to remove if you go whole hog. Now attach the felt so that the paper clip is sandwiched between the felt and accessory. Use the toothpick to push the felt tight against the paper clip and accessory. Allow to dry based on manufacturer's recommendation. If you're using E6000, you can pick it up (gently) in as little as half an hour just to check out your handiwork. Do not use for twenty four hours. Loctite works much faster but has some drawbacks as noted above. It is an incredibly strong bonding agent and if you need speed, go with Loctite.

4 When your fancy paper clip is fully dry, you can trim the felt so that it's not visible from the front but still gives the clip a polished look from the back.

TIPS

Please don't use Grandmother's good jewels. Costume jewelry from tag sales, old buttons, or jewelry from a dollar store reimagined will look fantastic. Also, if you're snipping any parts, safety glasses are absolutely necessary.

If you're making a fancy paper clip from a pin, you can gently press the felt into the back of the pin since the cardboard you inserted is rather pliable. Don't push too hard—gently nudge it in place with a toothpick or your fingernail.

4

Any paper clips that you steer clear of when making your creations?

I'm not a fan of paper clips with the non-skid feature. The non-skid component seems to just be a roughed-up paper clip, and while that does lend a certain amount of additional friction to hold the paper, it's aesthetically displeasing. Wow, I'm a paper clip snob!

Where's your favorite place to source paper clips?

Honestly, I find them everywhere, but the fastest place with the largest selection is definitely Staples. As an added bonus, they have an array of colors. I'm a fan of buying a small bag of plain black clips for many projects. Also, their gold clips have a really nice shine to them and the metal is especially strong.

How did you get started making fancy paper clips?

I had a collection that started about twenty years ago when I worked a 9–5 job in a corporate setting. Some lawyers really take their clips seriously, so when contracts came in with fancy clips, I'd nick the clip for my stash. Yes, I have a tin full of well-designed clips that I love, but I refused to use them. I'd just take them out and marvel at the designs. When I started using a planner I noticed that folks were embellishing their clips, and so I started experimenting with costume jewelry, military buttons, and even little plastic animal figurines.

You're a big fan of E6000 and Loctite glue. How did you come to favor them?

I tried using hot glue because I had a gun handy, but within a day or two the accessory popped off. Hot glue was too hard and brittle. I've used E6000 on other projects to great effect—even fixing my Mom's car door—so I tried that next. At the time, I couldn't find Gorilla glue in clear (that works well too) so I just stuck with E6000 because it hasn't let me down and I'm typically gluing metal to metal. Loctite is also incredibly strong, but I'm messy and typically get some on my fingers. Also, Design*Sponge and This to That have wonderful guides to adhesives if you're trying to marry two oddball components.

Make Your Own Planner

WITH THESE BASIC
BOOKBINDING SKILLS,
YOUR PLANNER COLLECTION
WILL GROW AND FLOURISH.

In this section you'll learn the basics of making your own planner from scratch using everything from beautiful fabric to old books to leather. The beauty of these projects (and nearly all in the book) is that you can scale them up or down by using what you have on hand—items from dollar stores or break-the-bank luxury supplies. Sometimes, you'll even find those break-the-bank items in a thrift store. Jean found Hermes sheets for $5 in a thrift store. Search high! Search low.

Skill Level: *Beginner* • Budget: *$10–$20*
Time: *1–2 hours*
Contributor: *Amanda Hawkins*

Repurposed Book Binder

SUPPLIES NEEDED:

HARDCOVER BOOK

INEXPENSIVE OR USED NOTEBOOK WITH BINDER MECHANISM THAT FITS INSIDE SPINE OF CHOSEN BOOK

2 ($^1/_8$-INCH) SEX BOLTS (AKA BARREL NUT, BARREL BOLT, CHICAGO SCREW, POST AND SCREW, OR CONNECTOR BOLT)

MATTE SPRAY ADHESIVE OR DECOUPAGE GLUE (SUCH AS MOD PODGE)

SLOTTED SCREWDRIVER

PLIERS

SCISSORS

CRAFT KNIFE (SUCH AS AN X-ACTO KNIFE)

AWL (OPTIONAL)

Instructions

Remove the binder mechanism from the existing notebook. Cut away the binder so that only a small piece remains around each connector. Using a slotted screwdriver, pry the brad away from the binder and carefully twist it apart.

1 Using a craft knife, carefully remove the interior pages from the spine of the book by slicing through the crease of the endpapers. Scrape off any old glue that remains and trim rough edges from the cover. If the book has decorative endpapers, leave them attached to the inside of the book cover, removing only the block of interior pages from the center. Be careful not to cut through the cover itself.

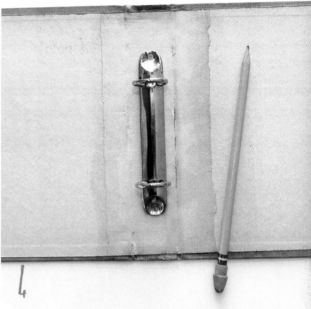

3 Pull off a single page from the interior pages and cut it to cover the inside of the spine, leaving an inch or so of paper on each side. If there are decorative endpapers, trim both so that they fold in together and cover the spine. Use adhesive to attach the paper to the spine. While the glue is still wet, close and open the book to create folds.

4 Center the binder mechanism on the inside of the book spine. Use a pencil to mark through the holes in the mechanism where the connectors will go on the inside of the spine. Set the mechanism aside, and then use a craft knife or an awl to create two holes just large enough for the screw to push through.

5 With the binder mechanism back in place, push the screws in from the outside of the spine and through the holes of the mechanism. Thread a bolt onto each screw, tightening the bolts inside by hand. When snug, hold the bolt with pliers while you use a screwdriver to tighten the connector from the outside.

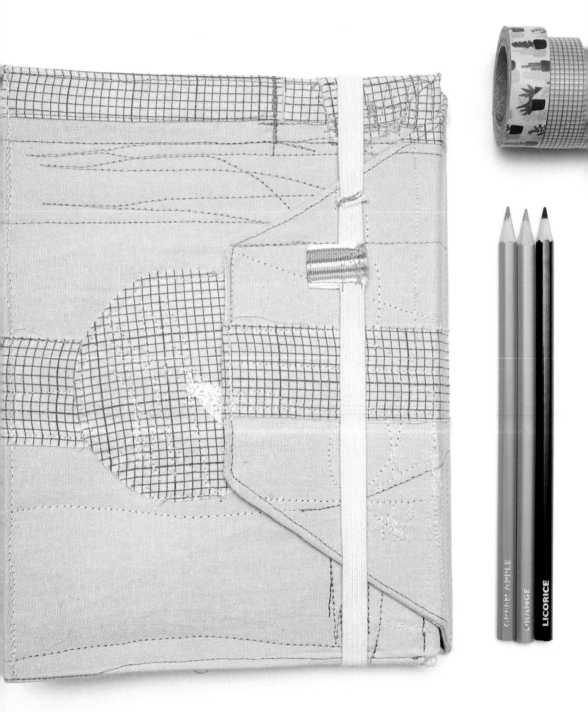

Skill Level: *Intermediate* • Budget: *$10–$20*
Time: *3–4 hours*
Contributor: *Amanda Hawkins, inspired by
Mary Ann Moss's Remains of the Day journal*

In Stitches Fabric Binder

SUPPLIES NEEDED:

FABRIC

*THIN PRESSED CARDBOARD
OR CARDSTOCK*

*INEXPENSIVE OR USED
NOTEBOOK WITH BINDER
MECHANISM*

*2 (⅛-INCH) SEX BOLTS
(AKA BARREL NUT, BARREL
BOLT, CHICAGO SCREW,
POST AND SCREW, OR
CONNECTOR BOLT)*

*SEWING MACHINE WITH
HEAVY-DUTY NEEDLE*

SLOTTED SCREWDRIVER

PLIERS

SCISSORS

*CRAFT KNIFE (SUCH AS AN
X-ACTO KNIFE)*

AWL (OPTIONAL)

ELASTIC

To create a planner that holds 8½ x 5½-inch paper, the front and back cover will be 7 inches wide with a 1½-inch spine. For the flap to cover half the binder when closed, extend the back cover by 3½ inches. Add the width of both covers, spine and flap to determine the full width of your cardboard. In this case, it is 19 inches wide. The height needs to be about half an inch taller than the paper, 9 inches in this case.

Instructions

Remove the binder mechanism from the existing notebook. Cut away the binder so that only a small piece remains around each connector. Using a slotted screwdriver,

2A

pry the brad away from the binder and carefully twist it apart.

2B

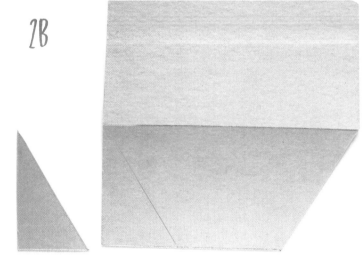

2 Insert paper into the detached binder rings to determine the width and height of your binder. Measure and cut your cardboard. Gently score the folds using a craft knife, making sure to leave width in the spine for the binder mechanism and extra on the right for a flap. You can

4

5

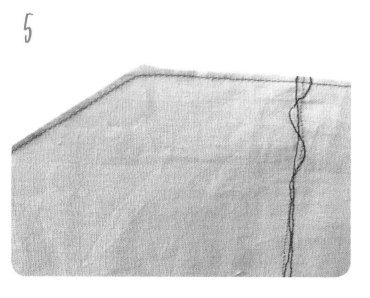

cut the corners off the flap to create an envelope-style closure.

3 Cut two pieces of fabric the size of your cardboard with 1 inch or more around the edges. These two pieces can be quilted, collaged, appliquéd, or simply left plain.

4 Sandwich the fabric with the right sides together, and then trace

the outline of the cardboard onto the wrong side of one of the pieces of fabric.

5 Pin the two pieces of fabric together and sew directly on the traced line, leaving one end open. Trim the excess fabric.

6 Turn the journal cover right-side-out and slide your cardboard inside.

7 Sew around the edges, making sure to stitch through the fabric and cardboard. On the unsewn end, tuck the raw edges of the fabric inside tightly as you sew.

8 To reinforce the structure of the spine, sew along the outer edges of the folds while they are closed. This area will be thick, so use the hand wheel in the beginning and sew slowly. Be sure that you are using a heavy-duty needle.

9 Decorate the cover by sewing on extra fabric or paper and other collage elements. Lower the sewing machine feed and scribble or draw on the fabric by free-motion sewing, using a contrasting color of thread.

8

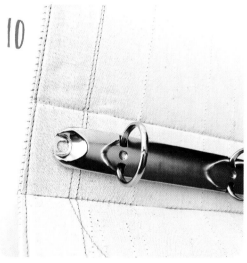

10

10 Place the binder mechanism on the inside of the book spine. Use a pencil to mark through the holes in the mechanism where the connectors will go on the inside of the spine. Set the mechanism aside, and then use a craft knife or an awl to create two holes large enough for the screw to push through.

11 With the binder mechanism back in place, push the screws in from the outside of the spine and through the holes of the mechanism. Thread a bolt onto each

screw, tightening the bolts inside by hand. When snug, hold the bolt with pliers while you use a screwdriver to tighten the connector from the outside.

12 Create an elastic band to hold the binder closed by sewing the ends of a short piece of elastic together and decorating with stitches and ribbon.

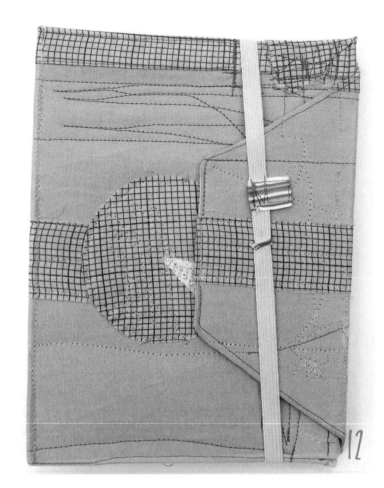

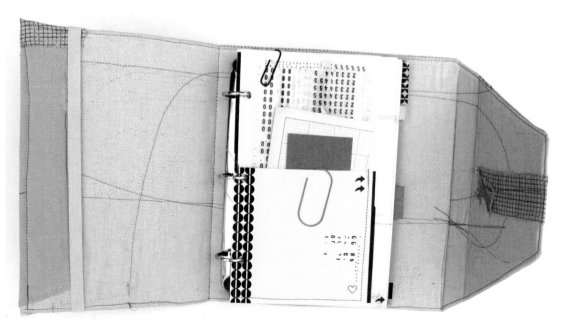

ABOUT THE CONTRIBUTOR

In 2007, **AMANDA HAWKINS** started creating planner templates and sharing them online at ahhh-design.com. Inspired by the idea of using planners as an art form, she started creating binders and templates in unique ways to make planning and note-taking more fun and creative. When she's not making plans, Amanda can be found playing with her kids, listening to music, painting, building websites, and dreaming of road trips to the beach.

Your project has such artistry. Did you formally train or are you self-taught?
A combination of the two! In the years since graduating with my Bachelor of Fine Arts in Graphic Design, I've taught myself new methods and techniques. I'd say my art changes and evolves constantly.

Is there a particular element, tool, or step in your project that is a favorite of yours? Or perhaps one that you dread?
I enjoy the whole process, but I truly love when a notebook is finished and it's time to fill it with paper, planner templates, and hand-cut dividers. I have a huge collection of random paper clips, paper scraps, tape, and stamps, so it's fun to dig through it and see what works. With the fabric binder, my favorite part is when it's time to

free-motion sew and decorate the cover.

You're a fan of two-prong binders. Any particular reason for that?
When I first started making planners and binders I was making them in an index card format, inspired by Merlin Mann's Hipster PDA. You could find index card binders with two-prongs at any office store for about $3. Since I was writing DIY tutorials online, the materials needed to be readily accessible to anyone. I also wanted the holes in the paper to be a standard size so a special hole punch wouldn't be needed. For my own planner, though, I'm a fan of disc-bound because it lies flat and the cover can be turned to the back like a spiral notebook.

Because of the nature of your project, we have to ask, who are your favorite artists?
Sabrina Ward Harrison, Teil Duncan, Heather Day, Heather L. Murphy, Massimo Nota, Mike Okay, Mark Rothko, William Kentridge, and a gazillion more. I love anything abstract and full of texture. Jen Simmons, who is pushing art with CSS. Textile artists Kate Loudoun-Shand, Jae-Young Eom, and Emily Fischer. Planner and book artists Patrick Ng and Sebastian Alvarez.

Traveler's Notebook Cover and Insert

This tutorial is for a cover that will hold 4–6 notebook inserts that measure 4 ⅓ inches wide x 8 ¼ inches tall, but you can adjust the size with the formula below.

Traveler's Notebook Measurement Formula

TO CALCULATE WIDTH OF COVER:
(Width of closed notebook insert + 1 ¼ inches*) x 2 = width of cover
*Adding the 1 ¼ inches allows for adding more inserts in your cover. If you only want to hold 1–2 inserts, you may want to only add ½ inch or ¾ inch to the width.

TO CALCULATE HEIGHT OF COVER:
Height of notebook insert + ½ inch = height of cover

FOR THIS TUTORIAL:
Notebook insert size (closed): 4 ⅓ inches x 8 ¼ inches tall
Cover height: 8 ¼ inches + ½ inch = 8 ¾ inches

FINISHED COVER WIDTH:
4 ⅓ + 1 ¼ = 5 ½ inches
This is the width of the closed cover. To find the open measurement, multiply it by 2.
5 ½ inches x 2 = 11 inches wide

COVER DIMENSIONS:
Open: 11 inches wide x 8 ¾ inches tall
Closed: 5 ½ inches wide x 8 ¾ inches tall

SUPPLIES NEEDED:

SCISSORS
PENCIL/FABRIC MARKING PEN
SEWING MACHINE
RULER OR YARD STICK
HEAVY DUTY DOUBLE-SIDED FUSIBLE INTERFACING (I USED PELLON 72F TWO-SIDED FUSIBLE ULTRA FIRM STABILIZER)
COTTON QUILTING FABRIC FOR COVER EXTERIOR AND INTERIOR
THREAD IN COORDINATING COLORS
CLOTHES IRON WITH STEAM OPTION/IRONING BOARD
5 GROMMETS
GROMMET MACHINE OR GROMMET TOOL (FOUND AT CRAFT STORES OR ONLINE)
2 YARDS OF 2MM ELASTIC CORD (FOR SPINE ELASTICS AND WRAP-AROUND CLOSURE)
CHARM
OPTIONAL: MATCHES/ LIGHTER, ROTARY CUTTER, SELF-HEALING MAT

143

Instructions

1 Measure and cut interfacing and fabric. Cut interfacing to size based on the formula. To measure fabric, use the size of the interfacing and add one inch to the width and height. Cut one fabric piece each for the interior and exterior.

2 Place the exterior fabric facedown on the ironing board and center the interfacing on top of it. The interfacing has adhesive on both sides, so it does not matter which side you place on the fabric. Trim off the corner of each edge of fabric. Following the instructions for your interfacing, set your iron to the appropriate temperature. Fold the fabric of each corner over the interfacing and place the hot iron on fabric for 3–5 seconds to adhere it to the interfacing. Be careful not to run the iron over the interfacing itself as adhesive will stick to the iron plate.

1

2A

2B

2C

3A

3B

4

4 Place the right side of the interior fabric facedown on the ironing board and center the interfacing onto the fabric, with the exterior fabric facing up. Trim the corners as you did with the exterior fabric.

Then, carefully flip over the two pieces so the interior fabric is now facing up. Quickly run the iron over the center of the rectangle, staying away from the edges. This will adhere the fabric to the interfacing so it will not move as you work on the edges.

3 Starting on a short side, fold the fabric over the interfacing and place the iron on the fabric for 3–5 seconds to adhere it. Working in 4-inch sections, continue to fold the fabric edge over and iron down. When finished, fabric should be smooth and adhered around the edges.

5

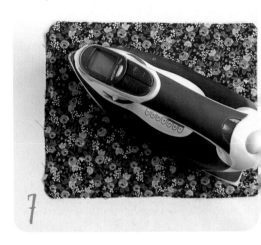

7

6

ric peeking out. The goal is to create a nice straight line with crisp folded fabric along the edge. Working in 3-inch sections, iron the edges on the three remaining sides. To finish the corners, fold each side to create a point.

5 Fold each trimmed corner section of interior fabric under approximately ¼ inch so that you see about ⅛ inch of the exterior corner. Press each corner in this manner.

6 Starting on a short side, fold the fabric under approximately ⅜ inch so that you see about ⅛ inch of the exterior cover fab-

7 Follow the manufacturer's directions for your interfacing and press the entire rectangle with the iron. Flip to the other side and repeat to adhere the fabric on both sides.

8 With the interior fabric facing up, sew a line of top stitching around the edge of the cover with coordinating thread. Fold the cover in half. It will be stiff due to the interfacing. Depending on the design, you can choose which side you want on the front cover.

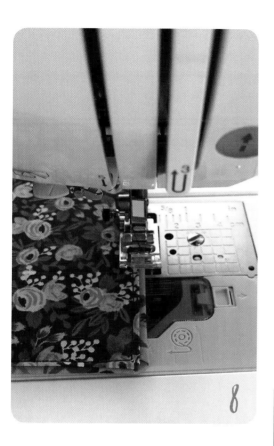

8

9

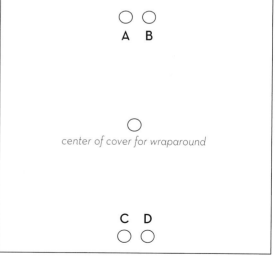

A   B

center of cover for wraparound

C   D

9 Measure and mark five grommet holes with a pencil or fabric marking pen. The center grommet should be located in the center of the cover. When you fold the cover closed, the grommet should be along the center of the spine evenly spaced between the top and bottom edges. The top and bottom grommets should each be ½ inch from the edge of the cover and be spaced ½ inch from each other. (See diagram at right.) Apply the grommets according to the manufacturer's directions.

10 String the elastics through the grommet holes following the diagram. Follow this order: A, B, C, D. With the interior facing you, string one strand of elastic down

TO HOLD SIX NOTEBOOKS

Using two 12-inch pieces of elastic, tie the ends together to create a loop. This will create a band that you can use to hold two notebooks together.

Slide the elastic through the center of two notebooks and close each notebook. They will be attached. Then slide one notebook under one of the elastics in your traveler's notebook. This will allow you to hold additional books.

through A, up through B, down through D, up through C. Tie a knot and trim the excess. Repeat for the remaining strand(s). To prevent fraying, carefully run a flame over the elastic tips.

Depending on the size of the grommets, you may be able to hold 1–3 strands of elas-

tics. The ones I use are $^{11}/_{64}$ inches in diameter and comfortably hold two strands, which will hold four notebooks.

11 For the closure, string the charm onto the elastic, which will keep it from falling out of the grommet. String the two ends up through the center hole on the cover and tie a knot on the interior side. Close the cover and test the closure to make sure it is not too tight or too loose. Adjust as necessary and trim the ends. Run a flame over the tips to prevent fraying.

Skill Level: *Beginner* • Budget: *$5*
Time: *30 minutes*
Contributor: *Kristie Cain*

Notebook Insert Tutorial

Instructions

1 Determine the size of notebook insert you want to make. This tutorial is to make an insert 4 $\frac{1}{3}$ inches wide x 8 $\frac{1}{4}$ inches tall (closed). Cut the paper and cardstock to the desired size with a paper cutter. Remember to consider the measurement of the insert when open. In this case, the width is 8 $\frac{2}{3}$ inches.

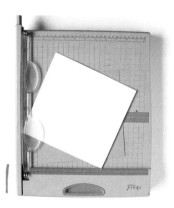

SUPPLIES NEEDED:

10 SHEETS OF PAPER (CARDSTOCK, WATERCOLOR PAPER, COPY PAPER, OR ANY YOU CHOOSE)

1 SHEET CARDSTOCK

LONG ARM STAPLER

BONE FOLDER

RULER

ROTARY CUTTER

PAPER CUTTER

SELF-HEALING MAT

2 Crease the sheets of paper and cardstock in half. Run a bone folder along the crease to ensure a clean fold. Assemble the paper and cardstock and use the bone folder to reinforce the crease.

3

4

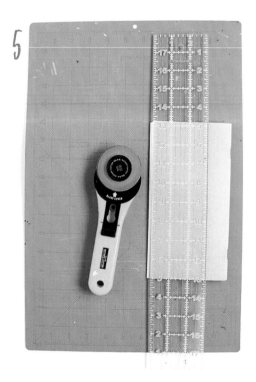

5

3 Open the insert and staple it twice along the outside spine (on the fold), about 1/3 of the way from the top and 1/3 of the way from the bottom.

4 Run the bone folder along the closed spine to create a clean fold.

5 To cut off paper that extends outside of the cardstock cover, place a metal or acrylic ruler on the edge of the cardstock and cut off the remainder using a rotary cutter. This will create a clean, professional insert. Decorate to your heart's content.

About the contributor

KRISTIE CAIN is the owner and maker of Gold Standard Workshop, a small creative business based in Seattle, Washington. She creates handmade fabric traveler's notebooks and related planner goodies. She often spends her weekends meandering through estate sales looking for her next project.

How long have you been sewing, and what or who inspired you to start?
My mother gave me a sewing machine for Christmas about ten years ago and I've been sewing on and off ever since. We've always been a crafty family, and she made a lot of my clothes and Halloween costumes growing up.

You're a big fan of Rifle Paper Co.'s fabric. What other fabric and patterns set your heart on fire?
I adore all fabric lines that Cotton and Steel produce—it's modern, colorful, and in line with my style. As far as other patterns and fabric, I buy what speaks to me, but I love florals and bold black-and-white designs.

Tell us a bit about how you use your planners. Are you thematic or do you go with dated/chronological?
Since traveler's notebooks allow for mul-tiple interchangeable inserts, I have thematic to-do and brainstorm lists for my online shop, and separate weekly and monthly inserts to help me keep track of goals and deadlines. No bullet journaling yet, but I do love using dot grid inserts.

Have you ever made one that's so dear you've been unwilling to use it?
No, but I have made some traveler's notebooks that I like to lovingly stare at from time to time because they're just so pretty.

Admit it, you hoard fabric like everyone else, right?
Absolutely. I hoard fabric and paper in my tiny one-bedroom apartment. The good news is that now I have the excuse that I can use the fabric for my business, and I must buy that pattern for my customers.

Anything else you'd like to share about your process?
Traveler's notebooks are not difficult to make, but there are a lot of steps to the process. Don't let that discourage you! At the end, you'll have an insanely useful cover that can be used for years. And they make great gifts too!

Skill Level: *Intermediate* • Budget: *$20*
Time: *3–4 hours (not counting drying time)*
Contributor: *Dawn DeVries Sokol*

Painted Canvas Journal/Planner

- CANVAS FABRIC OR HEAVY MUSLIN
- GESSO, WHITE OR BLACK
- CATALYST WEDGE OR AN OLD CREDIT CARD
- RULER
- ELASTIC THREAD/CORD
- SCISSORS
- AWL OR JAPANESE SCREW PUNCH
- GLOSS MEDIUM AND VARNISH OR SPRAY FINISH
- SANDPAPER
- ACRYLIC CRAFT PAINTS
- MICRON PENS FOR DOODLING/LETTERING
- ACRYLIC PAINT MARKERS (I USE LIQUITEX OR MONTANA BRAND—THERE ARE SEVERAL SIZES OF TIPS AVAILABLE)
- SPRAY PAINTS/STENCILS (OPTIONAL)
- RUB-ON TRANSFERS (OPTIONAL)
- RUBBER STAMPS AND INK

As an art journaler and mixed media artist for about thirteen years, I've made my share of journals. When I traveled to London and Dublin in 2009, I was determined to make a journal I could take with me that would be flexible, thin, and easy to make. You can make this same kind of cover and turn it into your daily planner using the insert tutorial on page 149. The structure is similar to the Traveler's Notebook but doesn't require sewing.

Instructions

Determine the finished size of your journal. This project will show how to make a 5¼ x 8½ inch cover (closed).

Cut the fabric or heavy muslin to an 11½ x 9½ inch piece.

1 On one side of the fabric, spread gesso with a Catalyst wedge or old credit card. Make sure to cover every bit of fabric with gesso, as it will prime the piece for paint. Once dry, flip the fabric over and gesso the other side. Let dry thoroughly.

3 With acrylic paints, paint your cover. I used craft-grade acrylic paints and spread a few layers of color over each side with the Catalyst wedge. Make sure to paint all the way to the very edges of your canvas piece and spread the layers evenly and not too thick. Let the cover dry completely.

TIPS FOR DECORATING YOUR COVER

- Choose a color palette that you love or evokes the mood or purpose of your planner.

- Craft paints will work just as well as more expensive paints. I prefer water-based acrylics and use various brands together.

- If using non-toxic paints such as craft paints, do some finger painting! You can also wear rubber gloves or apply a product like Glove in a Bottle beforehand to protect your skin.

- Rub-on transfers are an easy way to add letters, numbers, and different images.

- Add your own doodles or lettering to your cover to make the planner more personal.

- A pencil sketch can help in planning out the design of your cover. Once the fabric is gessoed and dry, you can sketch a design right onto the surface.

- Paint all the way off the edges of your fabric.

- Don't overthink or worry about the final result. Just have fun and enjoy the process!

4 Once the paint has dried, you can decorate it even more with acrylic paint markers or Micron pens for doodling and lettering, rub-on transfers, spray paints and stencils, and other embellishments. (See "Tips for decorating your cover.")

5 After your cover is designed and dried, flip the piece over so you're looking at the back, which will be the inside cover. You can choose to decorate this as well or leave it simpler. I like to paint or write my contact information on this side. Just make sure not to write it in the middle of the piece or it will get lost in the fold once you add in page inserts.

6 If you painted the inside cover, allow it to fully dry. The more coats of paint you layer, the thicker the cover will get, making it sturdier for use. Just be sure the paint dries thoroughly between each coat and you apply it evenly on each side so it won't crack when you fold it over. Four to five thin coats on each side should be sufficient. It should have a pliability and thickness similar to that of a Midori leather cover. If you are concerned about cracking in the fold, you can always add some fabric gaffer tape down the center where the fold will be (inside and out).

7 Using a rotary cutter or a heavy-duty cutter and straight edge, trim the edges of the canvas so that each side has a nice clean edge. Do this on a cutting mat atop a sturdy table. About 1/4 inch from each edge should be sufficient.

8 Brush or scrape a thin coat of Gloss Medium and Varnish over the front cover. (You can also spray the cover with a matte or gloss finish to minimize stickiness and possible smearing of marks you've made with pens.) Make sure to cover the edges of your cover with it as well so it won't fray. Let dry thoroughly. Do the same on the other side.

8

10

9 Once thoroughly dry, lightly sand both sides to take off a little of the gloss. This will also keep the cover from possibly sticking to other items.

10 If you have a heavy-duty corner punch—such as a Zutter—round all the corners of your cover. If not, use sharp scissors to round them out.

Lightly mark the center of the cover with a pencil. (I just fold the cover over and eye it!) Using a Japanese screw punch or awl, punch a hole in the fold about 1 inch up from the bottom (see "A" in diagram at right). Do the same at the top of the piece (B). Punch another hole halfway

D ○
B ○

A ○ | 1"
C ○ | ½"

12A

between the bottom edge and the bottom hole (C), and another one halfway between the top edge and the top hole (D). Now you will have four holes in the canvas as shown in the diagram on the left.

12 Pull a piece of elastic thread through the very bottom hole (from the inside out) and then through the hole above it (outside in). Run the thread up to the second to top hole. Pull through (inside out) and then back through the hole above it (outside in). Join both ends of the thread in the middle of the inside cover and knot. This will allow for two inserts. Snip off the excess ends of the cord.

Note: Refer to page 149 for insert tutorial. Make your insert ½ inch less in width and height to fit this planner. The second one will need to be made about a half inch shorter than the first.

Do you use primed canvas for this project? If not, can you tell us if we should prime the canvas? Will it make the canvas too stiff to bend?
I used unprimed canvas/muslin for this. Adding gesso primes the fabric. If you gesso a couple of thin layers on both sides, it stays bendable.

Can acrylics, oils, and watercolor paints be used for this project? Which do you prefer?
Acrylics are what I use mostly because of cost (there are a lot of great water-soluble craft acrylics). I've never used oils—they're too high maintenance. Watercolors are hard to manipulate and might not work as well.

The "2018" cover (page 152) has some collage. How do we add that?
I used a couple of old postage stamps and adhered them with gel medium. That's the beauty of this planner—you can decorate it any way you want.

You recently began drawing cats and dogs. How did you start?
I began by painting a dog a day and posting them on social media. You only get comfortable and have more fun with any art medium if you do it consistently. A publisher reached out to me and we published three board books: Good Dog; Here, Kitty, Kitty!; and Leapin' Lizards! I love painting pets because they're such a part of our lives.

Skill Level: *Intermediate* • Budget: *$20–$40*
Time: *1 hour*
Contributor: *Dawn DeVries Sokol, inspired by Teesha Moore at www.theartstronauts.com*

Leather Transfer Fauxdori

SUPPLIES NEEDED:

- 1 (3-5 OUNCE) PIECE OF LEATHER THE SIZE YOU WANT THE FINAL COVER
- AVERY INKJET IRON-ON DARK T-SHIRT TRANSFERS (03279)
- CLOTHES IRON
- ELASTIC CORD
- JAPANESE SCREW PUNCH OR HEAVY-DUTY HOLE PUNCH
- SCISSORS
- ROTARY CUTTER
- SELF-HEALING MAT
- STRAIGHT EDGE OR RULER
- IMAGE TO PRINT OUT ON THE TRANSFER
- ZUTTER CORNER ROUNDER (OPTIONAL)
- GEL MEDIUM (OPTIONAL)

I first saw these transfer "fauxdoris" (a term used for Midori planner imitations) from mixed media artist Teesha Moore. She showed how to make them on her subscription site, www.artstronauts.com. I wanted a planner I could make all my own, with my own design, but still with the feel of a Midori. It's incredibly easy and fun to see your design on leather!

Instructions

Determine the size you want for your cover. I designed my cover so that the transfer covers the entire area, edge

161

to edge. My final cover measures 7 3/4 wide (including front and back covers with a 1-inch wide spine) x 5 3/4 high. So the entire width = front cover + spine + back cover. Print out your image on the transfer according to the instructions on the package. I used one of my designs. (Use your own images and artwork, such as an old journal page, collage, or painting you've done. Do not violate someone else's copyright.)

1 Trim the image down to the size you wish for your cover. With a rotary cutter and straight edge, cut a piece of leather the same height and width as the transfer image, the width being twice the size you want your cover to be once it's folded.

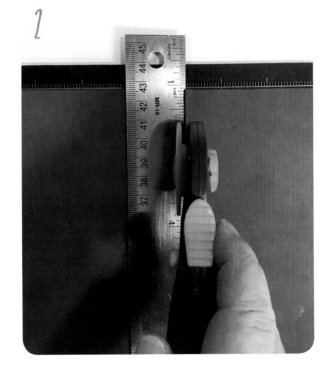

3 Follow all of the instructions for transferring the image to the leather with your iron. Do this on a solid surface such as a wooden

table or countertop, not an ironing board. Put a pillowcase down underneath the leather and a piece of tissue over the transfer image and leather. Don't put any water in your iron. Make sure not to move the iron around over the image, but to pick up the iron before moving it to another spot on the image. Iron all areas of the image to ensure transfer. Pull up the tissue. If the transfer is not

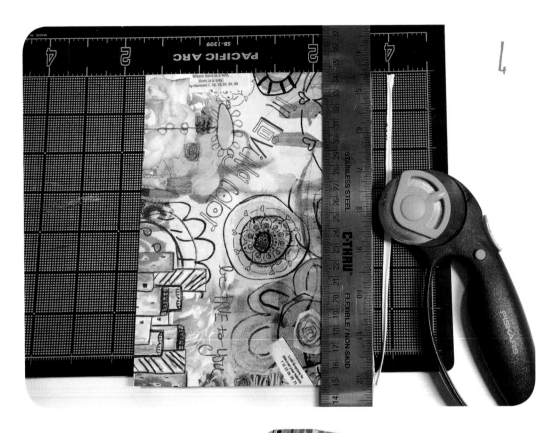

4

completely sticking down to the leather, iron that area again. Let the leather cool completely before the next step.

4 Once the image has trans-ferred, trim excess leather with a rotary cutter and straight edge. Use a self-healing mat to protect your table surface.

5

5 Using a Zutter corner rounder or scissors, round each corner of the cover.

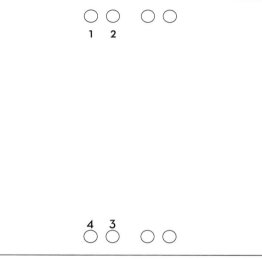

TOP

○ ○ ○ ○
1 2

4 3
○ ○ ○ ○

BOTTOM

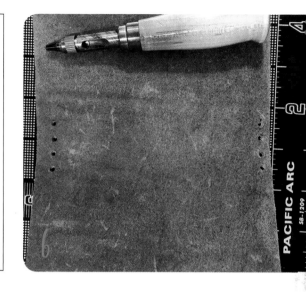

6 Fold the leather over to determine the spine area. (The width should be an inch.) Using a Japanese screw punch or heavy-duty hole punch, make two holes side-by-side, to the left of center, about ¼ inch down from the edge. Do the same to the right, and then make the same four holes at the bottom of the cover in the same way. (See diagram above.)

7 Cut a piece of elastic thread to be four times the length of the cover.

8 Pull the elastic thread through the inside out from the first hole at the top (1), then back into the cover

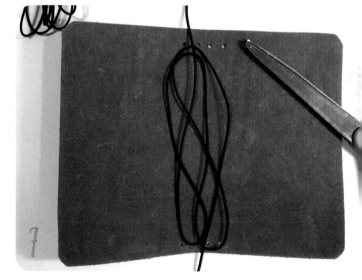

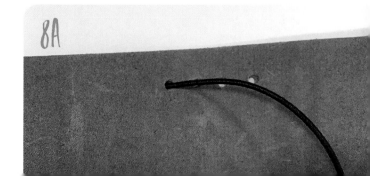

through the hole to the right (2). Now pull the thread to the bottom edge hole that lines up with the last hole at the top (3). Pull the cord through to the outside and then back in through the hole next to it (4). Join the two ends inside so you have two lines of cord side by side. This will hold two inserts. Do the same with the other four holes punched. You will have four lines of cord for four total inserts.

9 With the screw punch, make a hole in the center of the leather piece. Double a piece of elastic thread (the same length as the width of your cover), then pull the middle of the cord through the hole from

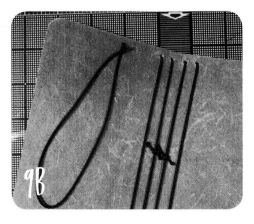

You're an artist who is known primarily for working with paper goods, paints, markers, etc. Was working with leather a challenging transition?
Not really. The leather I used wasn't as flexible as I would've liked, so I'd like to experiment with various thicknesses of leather. I took a leather bracelet workshop at a retreat once. We stamped into the leather and used watered-down paints to accent the pieces. It was fun, but I think I'll stick to making journals!

Any suggestions on where to source leather inexpensively and what to watch out for?
I have a couple of resources listed in the back of the book, but you can always use old leather items just as long as the leather isn't too thin or broken down.

Best fabric suggestions for our friends who prefer not to use leather. Will this work on faux leather?
I'm not sure that faux leather would work, as it might not take the heat of the iron so well.

Any suggestions for simple textured embellishments/stamps, like using a pattern tracing wheel or shaped cookie cutters?
Sure! You could also use metal stamps and a hammer to punch emboss letters or other designs. You could also use a heavy-duty sewing machine to sew along the edges for a nice finish.

the inside out. Make a loop large enough to slip around the whole cover. Knot the two ends of the cord inside. This will serve as an elastic enclosure that will wrap around the journal.

Note: I recommend carefully brushing a light coat of gel medium along the entire edge of the journal to finish it off. Do this with a small brush or the end of a popsicle stick. It should help keep the transfer from possibly peeling up as well as smooth out the edge.

Exposed Spine Planner

The final dimensions of your planner will depend on the size of the book board you use. Here we use a piece that is 8 ½ x 5 ⅝.

Instead of blank paper, you could use graph or lined paper to create a bullet or traditional journal.

Instructions

1 Plan the order of your pages and print your planner design onto the front and back of each sheet of drawing paper. Thirty-five sheets will accommodate thirteen months (i.e., January–January) and fifty-seven weeks, each covering a two-page spread. Your planner design is not required to go across a two-page spread; you may set it up however you prefer. Also, you can use fewer or more sheets of paper, as long you divide them evenly among the signatures (aka, a group of pages).

2 Fold each of the pieces of paper in half, aligning the shorter edges. Use the bone folder to burnish the creases.

SUPPLIES NEEDED:

- 36 (8 ½ X 11-INCH) PIECES OF DRAWING WEIGHT PAPER (GRAIN SHORT; THIS INCLUDES ONE SHEET TO USE AS A TEMPLATE)
- BONE FOLDER
- 2 (8 ½ X 5 ⅝-INCH) PIECES OF BOOK BOARD
- CUTTING SUPPLIES (UTILITY KNIFE, NON-SLIP METAL RULER, AND CUTTING MAT)
- 3 BOOK SPINES, EACH A MINIMUM OF ¾ INCHES WIDE (YOU CAN ALSO USE FOLDED BOOK CLOTH)
- GLUING SUPPLIES (SMALL BRUSH, PVA GLUE, AND WAXED PAPER)
- PENCIL
- AWL
- 1 (68-INCH) PIECE OF WAXED LINEN THREAD
- #20 OR #22 ROUND END TAPESTRY NEEDLE

3 Nest together five of the folded sheets to create a signature. Repeat until all of the folded sheets are nested into signatures. You will have seven signatures. Stack the signatures in order (top to bottom) and set aside.

4 Use a non-slip metal ruler and utility knife to cut the book board to size. Each cover will be the same height and $\frac{1}{8}$ inch wider than the folded pages.

5 Prepare the book spines. Use a craft knife to cut the spine from a book, cutting as close to the hard cover board as possible. This will leave about $\frac{1}{8}$-inch excess book cloth or paper from the hinge along the length of the spine. (Repurpose the rest of the book, if you can.)

6 Fold back the excess book cloth and use a small brush and pva glue to adhere it to the back of the spine. Repeat with the other two spines.

7 Create a hole punch template. Fold the remaining sheet of paper in half. Lay the book spines perpendicular to the folded edge of the paper, leaving a minimum of $\frac{1}{2}$ inch between the top book spine and the top edge of the paper and a minimum of $\frac{1}{2}$ inch between the bottom book spine

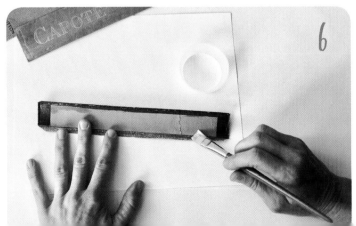

7

and the bottom edge of the paper. Use a pencil to mark the folded edge of the template at the top and bottom of each book spine.

8 Align the hole punch template at the inside of one partially open signature. Lay it on a cutting mat and use the awl to punch through all layers along the fold at each of the pencil marks. Remove the template and repeat, punching holes into all of the signatures.

8

9 A note on tension: It is important to keep the thread snug as you sew, but not so tight as to damage the paper. To begin sewing, thread about 3 inches of the waxed linen thread through the eye of the needle. You will sew with a single thread. Start at the inside of the first signature. Go out the top hole, leaving 2 inches of thread on the inside.

10 Place the top book spine perpendicular to the fold of the first signature, between the 1st and 2nd holes. Sew over the spine and down into the 2nd hole.

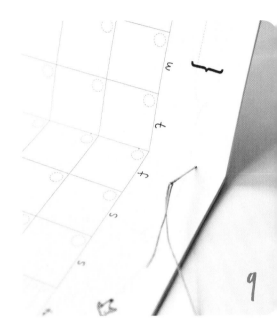

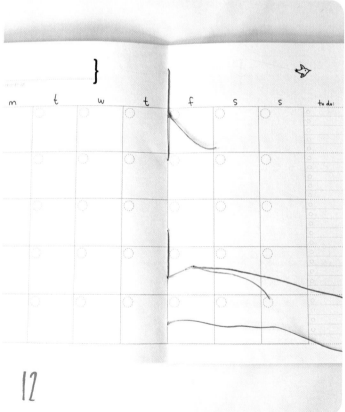

On the inside of the signature, tie the threads together directly over the 2nd hole. Go down and out the 3rd hole.

Place the middle book spine between the 3rd and 4th holes. Sew over the middle spine and down into the 4th hole. Go down and out the 5th hole. Place the bottom book spine between the 5th and 6th holes. Go over the bottom book spine and down into the bottom hole. Go up and out the 5th hole.

13

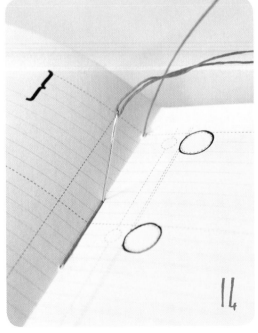

13 Add the 2nd signature behind the 1st and hold in place. Sew over into the 5th hole of the 2nd signature.

14 Go down and out the bottom hole, back up over the bottom book spine, and back through the 5th hole. Weave up and out the 4th hole, over the middle book spine, and up into the 3rd hole. Go up and out the 2nd hole, over the top book spine, and up into the top hole. Go down and out the 2nd hole.

15 Add the 3rd signature behind the 2nd. Sew over into the 2nd hole of the 3rd signature.

16 Go up and out the top hole of the 3rd signature. Go down over the top book spine and into the 2nd hole. Go down and out the 3rd hole, over the middle book spine, and down into the 4th hole. Go down and out the 5th hole, over the bottom book spine, and down into the bottom hole. Go up and out the 5th hole.

17 Add the 4th signature behind the 3rd and sew in the same way as the 2nd signature. Every even-numbered signature will be sewn in the same way as the 2nd (sewing up). Every odd-numbered signature will be sewn in the same way as the 3rd (sewing down).

18 Tie off at the inside of the 7th signature by passing the needle under the bottom stitch and tying the thread to itself over the 5th hole. Repeat to double the knot. Trim the remaining thread to ½ inch.

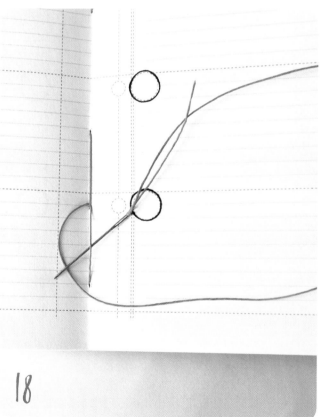

19 Adjust the book spines so that they are centered beneath the exposed stitches.

20 Attach the sewn book block to the covers. Hold the pages together with one hand and place the spine-side down on a piece of scrap paper. Place a piece of waxed paper between the covers and pages before gluing to prevent them from sticking together. (The waxed paper can be removed once the glue dries.) Apply a layer of pva glue to the back of the spines.

21 Align one cover board over the pages and pull the book spines tightly into place to adhere. Repeat to attach the book spines to the other cover. Wrap the entire book in waxed paper and press until dry.

ABOUT THE CONTRIBUTOR

ERIN ZAMRZLA is a bookbinder, designer, and teacher, and the author of *At Home with Handmade Books* and *Handmade Books for Everyday Adventures*. She loves to make things from paper and has been binding books for more than fifteen years. She works from her home in Los Angeles, California. See more of her work at erinzam.com.

We love how you used the spines of old books as part of the binding for the planner. How did you come up with the idea?
I'm always tinkering with repurposing materials into new books. At one point, I used the covers and pages from several discarded library books to make new journals. I kept the leftover spines "just in case." I eventually saw the potential to use them in lieu of tapes when trying out a new sewing technique.

Your binder uses a lot of repurposed materials. What are your favorite things to repurpose for creative projects?
Old filing and organizational materials are my favorite items to repurpose. They hold a particular nostalgia, as many of these papers have become functionally obsolete due to computers.

Some people think of books almost as sacred objects and hate the thought of taking them apart, even to use in other creative projects. Do you agree? Disagree?
I'm ok with repurposing books, as long as the finished product rivals the original in quality and purpose. I have my own collection of books that truly are sacred objects, and I wouldn't dare take them apart.

People often say that if you're going to write on good quality paper you should have an equally good pen. What are your favorite types of paper and pens to use in your planners?
I often use good quality drawing or sketch paper in my planners and cut them down to size. My absolute favorite paper to write on, though, is just about any Japanese sketchbook or notebook paper. I love the buttery smooth texture. My favorite pen for writing and sketching is the Pilot Hi-Tec-C. It comes in various tip sizes (I prefer the .4 or .5mm) and also takes refills. For a thicker line, I prefer the 1.0mm Copic Multiliner Pen.

Templates

By Hanna Andersson

- In this section you will find a few pages to include in your planner. You can copy the different pages as many times as you want and make copies for years to come.

- You can scan them to your computer and print them from there, or put the book in a copy machine and make copies of the pages you want to use. Then cut out and hole punch.

- If, for example, you want a pink calendar, print the copies on pink paper. For a more luxurious feel, invest in a thicker printer paper in a nice cream color.

- You can resize these pages to fit a smaller binder; just read the manual of your printer, or experiment. You can also print them to fit a bigger paper by choosing to print "fit to paper."

- If you don't want to use a ring binder, you can use a clipboard or file folder and do it the loose paper way, sorting them into sections by clipping them together with a paper clip. Tack the weekly calendar next to your desk area using washi tape so you can see your current agenda all the time. Then switch up when a new week comes around.

Things to do

date: _____

Work
- [ ] ....
- [ ] ....
- [ ] ....
- [ ] ....
- [ ] ....

Personal
- [ ] ....
- [ ] ....
- [ ] ....
- [ ] ....
- [ ] ....
- [ ] ....

Health
- [ ] ....
- [ ] ....
- [ ] ....

To get
- [ ] ....
- [ ] ....
- [ ] ....
- [ ] ....
- [ ] ....
- [ ] ....
- [ ] ....

Ideas

Keep in touch with

Name

Address

Country Instagram

E-mail Phone

Name

Address

Country Instagram

E-mail Phone

Name

Address

Country Instagram

E-mail Phone

Name

Address

Country Instagram

E-mail Phone

Copy at 100%.

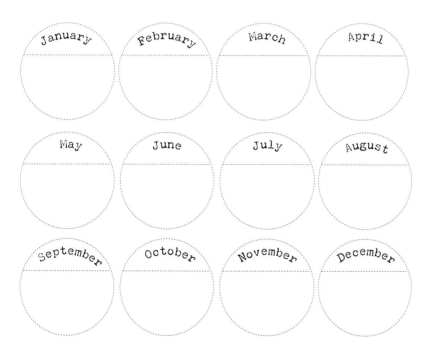

Monday	Tuesday	Wednesday	Thursday	Friday	Saturday	Sunday	Month:

January   February   March   April

May   June   July   August

September   October   November   December

Copy at 150%. Print on colored paper. Once you cut it out or punch it out with a 2-inch circle punch, add glue to the bottom half of the circle and then glue it to the back of your monthly overview page so that the month's name is sticking out on the top, or at the side of your planner for easy access.

Planner pages by Hanna Andersson, www.ihanna.nu

ABOUT THE CONTRIBUTOR

HANNA ANDERSSON, also known as iHanna online, is a Swedish blogger, artist, and writer who enjoys DIY-ing almost everything, including her own calendar, of course. She has made her planners from purchased and handmade notebooks, traveler's notebook inserts designed on the computer, and recycled books turned into ring binders. Hanna is a collage artist who has several 365-day projects under her belt, all documented on her blog—a place full of art, crafts, and creativity. She finds joy in painting and working in hand-bound art journals and altered books. She also enjoys her coffee with ice and writes for various magazines.

Find Hanna online on her blog (www.ihanna.nu), her Etsy shop (ihanna.etsy.com), or on Instagram (@ihannas).

You're so generous with your time on your blog. How long have you been blogging and which post gave you the greatest joy?
I started my blog in 2004, so I've been a blogger for a very long time in the internet world. I started writing a diary and taking photos when I was around eleven years old, so documenting my life has always been one of my favorite things to do. On my blog I write about my current creative passions, so even though I started out blogging about movies, knitting, and altering furniture, it has evolved to be a lot about notebooks, collage, journaling, and art these days. I don't have any favorite posts, but the kinds of blog posts that make me most excited to share are those that are about my art process, which is still evolving as I'm finding my way into becoming more and more an artist every day. I love writing about how happy creating makes me feel, and to try to inspire my readers to join me as I find time to create as often as possible in everyday life.

Can you tell us a bit more about the Postcard Swap you host?
A couple of years ago I started a do-it-yourself-postcard swap, where participants create ten handmade original postcards and get the same number back in the mail, from all over the world! I love mail art because it is a great way to push yourself to create, even when you're tired or feel rushed. It's a reminder of how far a little every day will take you and how important art is to us.

Right now I am hosting this swap twice each year, once in March and then sometime in the fall around September. We have people from every continent joining us and making beautiful mixed media mail art, sharing their creativity with the world. You can find out when and how to register on my blog www.ihanna.nu/postcard-swap. Everyone is welcome, whether you're a seasoned artist or a newbie who wants to give postcard swapping a try.

What's your favorite trick to organizing your art supplies?

As a messy artist who likes a little bit of everything from paper crafting to sewing to painting, embroidery, altering books, and crocheting, I can't really say that I have figured out what the secret to having an organized space is yet, other than keeping lots of transparent boxes on the shelves, reshuffling everything a couple of times each year, and not buying everything you think you need or want, but using what you have more than shopping. Sorting through materials is a great way to find inspiration too, so maybe there is a meaning to that part as well. Oh, and also, since I'm from Sweden, can I just say that I love the Råskog kitchen cart from IKEA. Mine is turquoise and called the Art Cart. It holds all my acrylic paints and I use it daily.

If you were to further personalize the templates you created for your own planner, what materials would you seek out? Glitter? Decoupage? Pen and ink?

For a luxurious feel I sometimes print my planner pages, especially tabs and monthly overviews that I reference more often, on a thicker, cream-colored paper (120 gsm), but any color of paper you like is fun to play with. I love to buy tiny Korean stickers via different Etsy shops to decorate my planner pages. I will use most pens and markers to write in events, especially neon gel pens, to underline and write in different colors. My own planner pages are almost always messy and a full range of rainbow colors, with kawaii washi tape where there is empty space, or flower doodles filling a whole week when I don't have any special plans or time to write in what I'm doing. I love going back and filling the empty spaces with lettering, doodles, or those cute stickers. I save wet media like paint and glitter glue for my art journal, but anything else is a go in my planner. I've also been making cute paper clip decorations with ribbons and beads that stick out at the top of your book.

Glossary of Terms

AWL: A pointed tool commonly used to make holes in leather and paper but can also be used to scratch or mark surfaces.

BOND PAPER: A high-quality paper often used for things like resumes and invitations.

BONE FOLDER: A flat, hard piece of plastic used to crease, flatten, fold, or burnish paper; originally made from bone, hence the name.

BOOK BOARD: A heavyweight paper board that acts as the structure for the front and back covers.

BRAD: A two-pronged fastener that allows you to gather multiple sheets of paper or other materials. Similar to a staple, but with a delightful button or other accoutrement on the surface.

BURNISH: To rub or polish something until it has a smooth finish.

CRAFT KNIFE: A sharp blade attached to a long handle; aka, utility knife, but more commonly referred to by the brand name X-Acto knife.

DECOUPAGE: A form of collage in which ephemera are cut from (typically) paper, glued to a surface (such as a box or table), and sealed with a varnish.

EPOXY: An adhesive composed of synthetic thermosetting polymers. With most epoxies, two matters are mixed together and react when joined to create a very strong seal.

EYE PIN: An eye pin is a long pin with a looped hook at one end. The loop allows jewelers to connect other pins or rings to it to create beaded chains or dangles.

FELT: A heavy, dense fabric historically made from wool. These days when people refer to felt they typically mean the synthetic felt, unless they specifically refer to wool felt. Synthetic felt is very inexpensive.

FINDINGS: Findings is a general term for the various metal components used when making jewelry or securing a bead or some other fanciful item to another.

FREE-MOTION SEWING: Sewing with the feed dogs lowered on a sewing machine in order to sew designs in any direction and not necessarily in a straight line.

GAFFER TAPE: Thick tape made from cloth that is used by gaffers (lighting technicians) on movie sets to tape down cords and cables to prevent tripping.

GEL MEDIUM: A thick colorless liquid used as an adhesive or protective finish.

GESSO: A thick, usually white liquid made from glue mixed with chalk or plaster, which is used to prepare canvas for painting.

GROMMET: A metal ring or eyelet used to reinforce a hole.

HEAD PIN: Similar to an eye pin, but with a flat head that prevents beads from falling off of it.

INTERFACING: A stiff material used between layers of fabric to give the material support and strength. Interfacing can be found in different weights and may also have adhesive on one or even both sides.

JAPANESE SCREW PUNCH: Two glasses of this and your planner goals will change! Just kidding. A Japanese screw punch is a type of hole punch used for punching through multiple layers of paper, fabric, or leather. (We're sorry it isn't a cocktail too.)

JUMP RING: A common component (finding) of jewelry making. It's a small ring that allows you to attach two items to each other. Some jump rings look like tiny keyrings and allow threading an item onto the ring in the same manner.

KRAFT PAPER: A strong, coarse paper (usually brown) frequently used in paper grocery bags or packaging.

LOBSTER CLASP: Literally looks like a lobster claw! A lobster clasp has a spring mechanism that allows you to hook something to another item via its claw, er, clasp.

MUSLIN: A cotton fabric woven using a "plain weave" or crisscross pattern.

PARACORD: Parachute cord/rope, often found in the cord or leather section of craft stores.

POLYMER CLAY: A malleable clay used for sculpting or modeling that is hardened by baking.

Primer: A preparatory paint that allows for a clean, smooth surface and blocks any background color.

PVA glue: Polyvinyl acetate; a water-resistant adhesive that dries clear.

Repurpose: To take an object and use it for something other than what it was originally intended, often with old or vintage materials.

Right side: The decorated or printed side of material, especially fabric.

Rotary cutter: A rotary cutter has a circular blade which allows you to cut fabric or paper with ease. It looks very much like a pizza cutter but thankfully has fewer calories.

Self-healing mat: Quite simply, it's a cutting mat that protects your table from the rotary cutter or craft knife.

Sex bolts: Also known as a Chicago bolt or a barrel bolt, it is a binding post screw that contains both a "male" and a "female" component. We'll let you figure out the rest. Plus it's clearly more fun to refer to by its common name "sex bolt."

Signature: A group of pages in a book or journal. Signatures are created from one large sheet of paper that is printed on both sides and then folded, cut, and bound.

Spread: The two pages that face each other when a book is open. Often, you'll see artwork or a scene spread across . . . the spread.

Transfers: Using an image (typically a mirror image) and transferring it to a surface such as leather, fabric, pottery, etc., generally by being rubbed on or ironed onto the target surface.

Transparency film: Clear plastic sheets that can be printed or drawn on so that you can trace or transfer images more accurately.

Washi tape: Authentic washi tape is made only from washi paper (a specialty paper made from plants native to Japan), and is transparent and repositionable.

Wrong side: The side without printed matter, or more easily understood as the back side.

Copyright, continued from page 4

Resources

About the Authors

JEAN SAGENDORPH is a twenty-year veteran of the entertainment industry. While at United Media, her clients included Food Network, *Peanuts*, *Fancy Nancy*, *Iron Chef America*, History Channel, Elf on the Shelf and more. From there, Jean launched Mansion Street Literary Management, a boutique literary agency that seeks exciting new authors and properties to represent. She spearheaded the creation of *Made with Love: The Meals on Wheels Family Cookbook*, which features recipes from renowned personalities like Martha Stewart, Helen Mirren, and more.

She is the author of *Starry Night*, *Hold Me Tight* and coauthor of *Icebox Cakes*. When not sewing something, gluing something, rehabbing a tiny lake house, or on www.petfinder.com, she can be found in her kitchen with butter, flour, sugar, chocolate, eggs, cream, and a rolling pin.

Always told she would be a writer, **DAWN DEVRIES SOKOL** earned a bachelor's degree from Arizona State University's renowned Walter Cronkite School of Journalism and Mass Communication. But she yearned to create visually, and soon worked her way from editing newspapers to art directing magazines, such as *America West Airlines Magazine*—from which a feature she art directed landed in *Print Magazine*'s 2002 Regional Design Annual. For ten years, she designed books for a wide variety of U.S. publishers.

Sokol's love of books evolved from designing to authoring. She began publishing titles focused on doodling and art journaling, including *Doodle Diary*; *Art Doodle Love*; *The Doodle Circle*; *A World of Artist Journal Pages*; *Year of the Doodle*; *Doodle Zen*; *Good Dog*; *Here, Kitty, Kitty!*; *Leapin' Lizards!*; and *Doodle Journeys*.

She also teaches journaling/doodling workshops on her blog and Creativebug.com. Her articles have appeared in magazines such as *Cloth Paper Scissors* and *Somerset Art Journaling*. Her journal pages and works on canvas and wood have been exhibited in books, on blogs, and in gallery exhibitions from Tokyo, Japan, to Tempe, Arizona, where she lives with her husband, TJ.

Acknowledgments

Many thanks (and cupcakes) to the numerous contributors who jumped on board, shared their wisdom, met the crazy deadlines, and otherwise joined our merry band. A big (gluten-free) cupcake to Michelle Witte, who helped keep us organized, herd the cats, and didn't laugh too hard when Jean changed the Dropbox password seven or eight times. Also, the lovely folks at St. Martin's Press, who showed great enthusiasm for this project. Thank you, BJ and Gwen.

We also wanted to mention how wonderful the folks at Rifle Paper Co., Field Notes, and Dylan's Candy Bar were when we reached out to them about using some of their items in the book. Their swift response and "go get 'em" attitude is what makes the creative community such a vibrant and welcoming group. Thank you so very much for your encouragement and belief in this project.

Jean would like to thank her mom (aka Momendorph), who has been championing the arts since forever and shares her stash without reservation. You're the best! Also, her whole family, who when she suggests "brunch and crafts" on a Sunday, shows up with a dish and happily sits down at folding tables to make all manner of weird and wonderful things. Who could ask for more? She is thrilled that Dawn agreed to coauthor this book. She's a dynamo. Her schematic is a work of art and she totally nailed it when Jean cobbled together a rough style board for the book—she made magic. And she's just flat out wonderful to work with.

Dawn would like to thank her husband, TJ, and her mom, who always support and encourage her creativity. She'd also like to thank Jean, her coauthor, agent, and cheerleader, who asked her to join her on this project. Jean, you're a great friend who always keeps me laughing—online, on the phone, and in person. I just wish we lived closer to each other!

Index